GRACE AT MIDWINTER

ALSO BY CLAUDIA JENSEN DUDLEY

The Fragrant Fire

In the Scale of Worlds (chapbook)

Waters of the Afternoon: A Song in Three Voices

GRACE

at

MIDWINTER

Poems
2000–2020

CLAUDIA JENSEN DUDLEY

Rasa Publications
San Francisco

Paperback ISBN 978-1-951937-68-3
Hardcover ISBN 978-1-951937-67-6

Library of Congress Control Number 2020919857

Cover design by Clara Dudley
Book design by Colin Rolfe

Rasa Publications
San Francisco

Distributed by Epigraph Publishing Services

For Bill,
who makes everything possible,

and for the Family Women
—aged 5 through 93—
a circle of Magic

Contents

Foreword

All births take place as an organic necessity. They are the appearance in this world of something new. This book, *Grace at Midwinter*, is no exception. Like many births, the time of its arrival was envisioned in a dream. The dream came in early February 2020. In this dream, I had invited everyone I know to a poetry reading in my home. Waking from the dream with a feeling of joy and certainty, I knew it was time to gather together the unpublished poems that had appeared during the last twenty years. But given the demands of life and energy—how?

Then came the pandemic, and the shutdown in March which ensued. In that new strange silence, in solitude, in the sudden lapse of demands, a thought returned to me. It had come through a loved one, quoting a great man: "*Only the impossible is worth doing.*" And few things seemed more impossible to me than this book. Impossible, it seemed, to put in order this large, unruly stack of poems, so different from each other, into anything coherent.

But as I looked through the poems, they both surprised and helped me. It seemed that not only were they a help to *me*—as though the reader were a different person from the writer—but that perhaps their time had come. I wondered whether they had been waiting to emerge at this moment of personal and general "midwinter"—a moment lacking so many supports and any pretense of a known future. And I realized that the dream had not lied; when the moment came to birth the book, our current technology would let me invite everyone I knew into my home.

So here are the poems. Not all of them will appeal to every reader, but it is my hope that their range can cover every taste—maybe even expand it. The different sections comprise poems in relation to a similar theme. Here is a kind of roadmap:

    •ᷤ *Whatever Is Living* centers on family life, the daily life close to us, its minute unfoldings.

    •ᷤ *The Singer Moving Everywhere at Will* celebrates language, language as incantation, a leap into other word-worlds.

    •ᷤ *Domestic Sequence* is a cycle of 32 haiku that appeared during a week in February 2007.

    •ᷤ *Occasional Crones, Elves and M.F.K. Goofrock* is meant solely for delight and laughter.

    •ᷤ *Approach to Magic.* Perhaps this can speak for itself.

    •ᷤ *Everything about Departure, A Lenten Journal,* and *Suite for Persephone* are three sections of poems that explore the mystery of death, and whatever we can know of rebirth and transformation.

    •ᷤ *The Holiday Annals of Frankie Catchild.* Did you think cats *couldn't* write doggerel?

    •ᷤ *Every Day Is a Living God of Time* is about a new beginning, a new look toward the scope of the work of our precious days.

    •ᷤ *The Peaches of Immortality* summons us out of the heart's deep winter, toward deepest light.

    •ᷤ The *Notes* at the end further clarify individual poems and their backgrounds, especially when they refer to myths, history, or bodies of ideas.

Sadly, this book is not accompanied by music as my earlier publications have been. Poetry is so often truly completed by music. But hopefully, these poems will carry their own music into the ears and psyches of those who read them. I hope they can be, just as they are, a help during these crucible processes of which we're now a part.

To put it very simply, may these poems fulfill whatever they were meant for. We would wish the same for ourselves.

Claudia Jensen Dudley
September 2020
San Francisco

GRACE AT MIDWINTER

Always new, this vigil we keep
the self dissolved in pain
with our lit candles at the threshold
obeisant to rain
of day and night, yields
ever to fire feeds
the bread we have always eaten
the spark and hope of reeds
but now, for the first time, tasted,
made whole and hollow both
as rough to the touch as golden
within the palm of earth
at our lips, received, the opening
we who are but the prayer
of sudden summer in the heart
breathed out the reed with air

Whatever is Living

BIG GIRL

"I'm a big girl now."
She's said it with pride for months.
Sleeps in a big girl bed. Talks, runs.
Eats raw carrots and nuts.
Is friends with her potty.

But yesterday at the park she watched
fifth and sixth graders laughing,
talking, teasing under the manzanitas.
And to the air, quietly, said,
"I'm not a big girl."

FIRST WAKING

First minutes one Sunday morning, sitting upright
in bed, not dreaming anymore. Letting
the lives of anyone who came to mind—
a Chinese farmer, a child in war, even
my atheist, prescient father—pass through.
Knowing this time was brief.
As though an ink brush flashed over a page
and much could be known, *had* to be known,
in a few strokes. And these others
were living, moving, speaking, illumined,
narrowed, touched. It wasn't just that we were part
of the same painting. We were the ink itself.

❧

CARING FOR A DEAR CHILD LATER IN LIFE

Soon she'll be able to walk, and I'll take her
down to my drought-dry lawn and we'll rake
the many layers of leaves already here by October,
remove the dry dying plants I'm too busy to water.
Time now runs slow, full and filled. But she
who is new and fresh, a challenge to the dead,
and even more to the fallow, asleep under the surface
in wait, is blessing to my sacrifice, to precious things
given up in mid-life, and most of all to that wind,
intelligent and unknown, before which at moments
I remove the protection of clothing and sit, exposed.

THE CHASM

He looks enough like her to be her son,
with his raccoon eyes, his stripes, his deep fur,
but how would she know? She never had kittens.
At his age, before she found us, she was probably
alone already, beginning to starve.
They don't understand each other.
Mateo, flying kitty, cat-grandchild, here
for his first Christmas ever, and Sadie,
eighteen, deaf, weighted and still,
ill with a bad cold since he arrived.

She is weary of defending her containment
from his tenderness and speed. She says,
"What will happen next? Why does he fly?
I have to share my home, but I will never
share my dish, my heating pad or my heart."

But Mateo, the fleet and long, fearless,
jumps onto the bed where she can't see.
Comes up from behind on her heating pad.
Puts one paw atop her brown head.
Says, "I can help. I am everything you're not."

But Sadie, from her deaf body, makes the sound,
the one note meant to penetrate
all the hearing world with terror.
Then she snarls and snarls, but does no more.

He finally leaves. She sinks back down
onto her pad, into a world withdrawn,
hard of breath, where few are loved.
It is a world, like ours, in which a heat source

is always preferable.
But if she must, she'll seek any hiding place
where Mateo cannot go,
even the cold winter porch.
To remember who she is.
To keep intact her full dignity and grief.

❧

GREASE STAINS

Restraint is a bird with a body
like clean glass. He cannot be seen
and leaves no traces. But for Christmas
he gave the woman grease stains
on her favorite tablecloth, visible forever,
after her daughter made salad there,
and drops of olive oil fell,
and the woman for once
kept quiet.

ASPIRATION

—for Leila at Six and a Half Months

Leila June sits up or lies flat, but would rather stand.
This is our grandmother's game, and has been for months.
I hold her standing—up, up and more up.
Her face is a whole moon grinning,
her feet on my thighs are brown birds,
mad light is in her eyes.
She stamps, goes forward, backward, to the sides,
is up, falls down, is up again,
is cockier each times, and tireless.
How could she know so soon
that this is what she's made for?
She can even forget, standing up,
that baby-costume she sees
in the mirror and can't take off.
(It is the only time she doesn't smile.)

She who ached to stand at eight weeks will,
like her grandmother, jump many guns.
But I wish her that leap into vastness sometimes
sparked by a long course in impatience.
Aspiration may change its colors and shapes,
but makes its home, gleaming,
on a steady spiral which never ends.
And Leila June, who loves mobiles, is dancing there.

FOLDING THE LAUNDRY

All dry it all comes out
his mine ours in wash
all warm to sort all wayward
socks grey black mine his
bath towels old
reliables
rags dear friends
skirts crying me
pants diffident
dishtowels eager
to help
napkins iffy

all that hands
fold hang put each
in place pile clump in wash
it all comes out all
the limp sprawled many
mixed still warm

but do sort please chaff
from wheat his mine
these that sheets shirts all
to closet drawer hook
rack with kith and kin

again through storm of water
fire air clean to poise
washed in wait
all each

for anything

FIRST DAY OF SCHOOL

As Greek Psyche and Russian Vasalissa sat
hopeless before the great mixed piles
of lentils, rice, barley, millet, told
to separate them out by morning or die,

I look out over four tables and eighty children
in this small bungalow, knowing only a few,
and a few more names. Wondering how I will ever
discern Lauren, Ori, Majigmaa, Louise, Rowan,
from Ariana, Hunter, Claire, Anaisa, Harrison,
and so many more. Knowing I must know, and soon,
who will make me laugh, who will fall headlong
into poetry, who will carry sorrow
from the mother or anger from the father,
who will shadow themselves in silence.
Wondering what it will take to meet each
in the land behind the eyes. Knowing
if we do not all rise together into feast-rooms
of the mind and heart, then none do.

Vasalissa's doll does her work in the night,
Eros sends an army of ants. Can I too
hold under my tongue the pellets
of magic that say *help comes?*

OF TODDLERS AND MEDITATION

You stay still on your cushion while she circles
the room, always moving, her blocks or soccer ball
or stuffed pink elephant in hand. Though you open your eyes
slightly when she comes close to you, just stands there.
Will she cry, pull your hair, hit your face?
No, she does none of these, she is only watching.
You stay still when she moves away again
to her drawer of toys, to the window or couch,
and even when she comes back, puts her gorilla book
in your open hands, walks off to the kitchen,
replaces the book with your water bottle.

But when she puts her arms around you
and holds you a long, long time, her heart
(as she stands and you sit) just touching your own,
your stillness breaks, your arms go out
and around her, and the sun of this world
enters you, perhaps forever.

MONDAY MORNING
(ACROSS THE WORLD)

Clara left home again on Friday, at 27.
Her bedroom door won't open this morning
or close again quickly to keep out the cats.
She isn't shivering, long-legged in grey shorts,
isn't bleary, morning-grumpy in the hallway.
And she won't leave her hair iron out,
won't boil tea water or rev up espresso.
She won't run out of her room at 8:20,
late for work, won't call for me to lock up.

Now her bedroom, doors still closed, her paintings
all around, glows luminous with their quiet,
their concentration of faces—all but her own.
Across the world she is seeking her fortune
of life and love—across the world.

So it's happening again.
That taste in the mouth, acrid.
Both taste and foretaste, inexorable.
And the need for a fifth chamber of the heart.

The Madwoman of Calcutta, a century ago,
was young and had lost her husband.
Stopped every young man in the street, asked,
"Are you *he*?" Years passed.
A neighbor saw her seated, aged, under a sacred tree.
Now radiant, hand on her breast.
"*He is here!*" she said, "*He is here!*"

EMILY SLEEPING

Emily in the night against the heart
could be any newborn baby.
But as flesh of your flesh, she is already
a half-familiar secret.
Time's night is a gift and she is sealing
herself into you, hour after hour.
It seems she knows fully who she is.

In her breathing and small heat,
the sleeping child composes herself.
She is the growing, the quickening
you yourself seek, she is already
the sung-to in the night. And in her own
soundless song, you are airlifted
out of the terrible trenches of the known.

And Emily sleeping is the sign
of herself leading toward you
as to world and time, as you in her
are toward the timeless.
What worlds are here, would clash here
in this living room looking down at a city,
over city lights, streets, poised
above sirens and sound?
But the worlds outside do not touch her.
Or perhaps, undisturbed, so deep
in her waking and sleeping, she enfolds
them too like a secret, half-familiar.

Her head on your chest moves with your breath,
her long hands and feet just touch you.
And you have left behind what you were.
There is nothing more to do
and you have stopped—
stopped long enough for once
to become complete
in the well of her silence,
in this whole that is loud and sweet,
though heard by no one.

᷿

LITTLE DANCER

Mozartian:
the rooms of her heart arranged
in play and love like tender wings, speckles
of light in late afternoon sun.

Little dancer in the park
or under the moon,
barefoot, hiding nothing,
birthday dancer,
childhood's butterfly
dark and magic in her body—

how
she is listening to dreams and fountains,
how
she is hearing the hush, always new,
of pearls, owls, stars, smiles. . .

INSOMNIA'S FRUIT

As night after night, the cage of sleep
blurred rain and wind outside
but did not obliterate them;
changed them into strange new demons
blotted with the blood of petty worries;
became heat and trembling,
the broken splinters of the spirit:

I saw that everything conspires to disperse the self,
and everything wishes the self contained.
Both are true.

Night is a friend only to the acquiesced, the watcher.
It asks for a yielding which is fruit, which jealously
guards the moments of a life with secret silence.
Grace in the night is a sword greater
than the anguish of the turning mind.
It dawns, shining, on the restive being.

I ask myself, "Who in you can reach
for that blade which is your own and lay it
in your bed, firm across your heart, and cool?"

It is for her that I write this poem.

HUMAN CONDITION

Baby won't take a bottle.

She's all smiles with herself, excited, her arms and legs
aleap in midair. Is there a chuckle?
Her blue eyes are on mine,
and between us the air
might crackle over with smiles.
With looking and dark-blue light.

Then I offer the bottle,
the battle.

It's mother's milk, which she knows, but she gnaws
her hand's edge, her knuckle, her thumb. Chooses
these over the milk of her mama.
Refuses my eyes.
Switches hands. Loses
her happiness to tears, anger,
shut cages of fatigue and hunger.

Hours pass.

And so close—manna.

IN JANUARY, MAY

—in January

January light.
My cats sleeping in the sun.
And they say death's real?

                      Is it true? Light plays
                      on this window web even
                      when I'm not watching?

Wounded butterfly,
who else hears your broken wings
flutter on asphalt?

                      Stay very quiet.
                      Something new has come to hear
                      all that "it" cannot.

—in May

Voluptuous May!
Oh world of petty doing
trampling you under!

Seeing as spiral.
Sudden, deeper and deeper.
The lush spring silence.

Is poetry dead?
No words for how cold May rain
surprises the weeds.

Are words leaving you?
And yet, this aging garden—
nothing more profuse.

What is this heartbeat
struggling to be heard above
a raging river?

END OF THE BEGINNING

Months after I wrote her name with a purple pen
on both her hands, and her mind and face were suddenly
wild with that knowledge, and she asked for "Leila"
on hands, feet, knees each time I saw her,
she is almost two now and proudly forages
in my sunroom for old markers, the purple ones.
Then covers her hands and face with lines of Leila,
pulls up pants, sleeves, blazons her legs and arms,
takes off socks and shoes, makes Leila on the soles
of her feet, spreads Leila all over her stomach.

And at night before sleep, she adds a momentous syllable
to the mantra of sacred names she recites by day:
"*No*, Mama, *No*, Dada, *No*, Baba, *No*, Nana."
And yet another, great with portent, "*Mine.*"
She plays, walks, looks, explodes with the world,
its syllables and names, hundreds of them now,
gathers all these in her growing pouch of power.
And armed with that power, sheathed
in her purple name like a young Egyptian god,
runs happily to the last remaining edge
of her formlessness and jumps.

THE NEW ROOMMATE

I asked the tall old elegant man, my friend's
new roommate in the nursing home,
"Please, what is your practice?"
Dark gurus sat in meditation on his walls,
Ganesha stood under his lamp,
rosaries and a fine wool cap hung on the bedpost.
Notes on the *Bhagavad Gita* lay open
on his bed, but the man wasn't reading.
He was staring at the wall, the window,
or maybe nothing.

His head turned when I spoke.
His gaze was blue, blue fire meeting mine,
which became, in my chest, like waves of water
after a stone, or like suddenly coming home.
He took my hand, said, "Sit down here and we'll talk."
I sat next to him, he began quietly
in his Polish accent. But his words soon broke,
sentences failed him. I listened, he stopped.

My friend's sister had said he rearranged
boxes and drawers in surprising ways,
wore her small sweater when she wasn't looking.
But she liked him. When the nurses came in,
he thanked them with two hands joined.
They smiled and joined their hands back.

I went to my friend, and for music
played Chopin nocturnes. The Polish man,
so still on his bed, sat looking down.
I had been in this room many times, but now,
around the three of us, around the music,

silence spread and circled like a new land.
My friend was sleeping as I left, and I asked
his roommate, did he mind the music on?
He looked up at me, radiant, saying:
"You can hear that again and again,
and it will always be well with you."

ON ANNE'S 29TH BIRTHDAY

Irises fading on my table, and Anne is 29.
Last night at dinner, at sunset, she sat carrying
our first grandchild in her body, under green shawls.
The four of us were in the restaurant after rain.
We were watching the Bay, dessert had just come,
and Anne was unwrapping her gifts, when
our men saw, in that perfect dusk, red lights
on the bridge; something bad was happening there.

But I sat facing Annie, seeing
there was nothing and everything I could do to help.
It is the moment of unwrapping every gift,
it is the moment someone is dying or hurt.
And we are all together now, but not always. . .

And this morning, it seems even these irises,
quiet tea, treading cat on my papers and books,
and possibly rain again today, on Anne's birthday,
are composed of waiting. Are preparation, reparation.
And there is nothing and everything to help.

And the unfolding is a room or a sea
so walless, so deep, that for a moment
I consent to swim without seeking land.

LEILA PLAYING WITH SAND

Leila's small hands and feet are in the sand,
she has touched sand before but now, again,
it is a meditation, her eyes are wide, watching it,
she is still but for hands and feet over
and under and in it, it is more important
than swinging or smiling, it is the moment's all,
each cell-stone of sand an all, and all together
a variegated streaming with asteroids
of pebbles, dried wood between her fingers,
each handful a moving of time and earth,
a never-running-out. And she

is burying her foot and finding it, softer
than before. She is raising and lowering
whole handfuls, letting them fall so slowly,
closing her fingers, opening, measuring,
listening to rivulets of sand, the whole world
between fingers and toes. And she is upon it,
the sand upholds her, it is only the beginning.
And over the sand-world she, in her stillness and awe,
is the one mover—the maker.

EMILY, ALMOST TWO, LOOKING AT MIRRORS

That what she sees
in every mirror she seeks
is not herself, yet is,
she comes to learn.
And marvel on.
Wall mirror or the ones she holds
in hand, it is the same.
She looks to see if anything
has changed between her peerings. Is she
again herself? And now, is she
disarmed or comforted,
or yet amazed?

The stark dichotomy of seen and felt
will flame, if she is lucky, into wonder.
And wonder may yet weave
into the secret silk of deep inquiry.

That all the named, the seeming-seen—
the kitty, ant, tree, friend, all—
peer out yet live inside, unseen,
as she does; that form in the mirror
threads onward, a river, as she is;
that form is never final, nor is she:

could change
and go on changing her
forever.

WHAT STIRS AT THE LIPS

—for Robert and Martha, November 21, 2009

It is because you are becoming flames,
while seeking to grow both root and wing,
that you are entered, invited by hosts unseen
into the treasure house of moments:
ruby light, the emerald of faces, amber of touch.
All edible jewels, awaiting you.

It is because you have found each other, yet are only
loaned to each other;
and because limbs, voice, scent,
the dear footfall at day's end,
are in space and time all finite:
you must pass into the mastery of love
through the mystery of leaving. While humility
keeps her sacred stone in your shoe.

And as we rise up alone, as two, or as many,
before the open sea of the unknown,
we partake ever more deeply
of the shelter of the body.
There to be home for each other only
as well as to willingly rejoin
the generosity of that living loam
in which all wounds, everywhere, are tended to.

How gladly the lovers' day, each day, rounds itself,
into one whole, new and new,
tapping your limbs and worlds for liquid gold!
At the secret table of the heart, what you seek and sing
spills over into open air, redeems profoundly

both future and past. And what stirs at the lips
is imbided at the source, where intimately you are blessed.
And the source is your savoring—your flowering guest.

❧

GRATITUDE

That the power went out winter solstice night, and Bill and I
drank wine with red candles lit all around, and the teenagers,
Clara and Keith, went out for a walk in the dark,
and came back after she called him Attention Whore
and he stopped talking in words but used furious hand gestures
in the candlelight; and Anne's friend Lillie, alone at home
across the park, drove slowly over to our house and they walked
to Clement Street, tenderly hopeful the Irish bars
had not lost power; and Bill and I, alone and wry,
knew that if we tried to make love, they'd all come back,
and if we didn't, there would be all the time in the world.
So we let our cat Sadie steal his chair, and then his lap,
and then mine, and told again what we most loved
about the other (lest it be forgotten),
or in case it had recently changed.

BACK IN SOUTHPORT AGAIN

Now so many Yankees have moved down this way,
without drawls and slim-bodied,
that they stand out even from afar
in the WalMart across the gully.
The natives tend to the heavy or bone-thin,
are often sad-eyed. But most folks here smile easily,
would give you their place in line,
carry food to their neighbors, new or sick,
and on Sundays fill every church in town.

The WalMart here is different from out west:
whole aisles for knitting needles and yarn,
for pastries, white bread, oversized clothing,
and more dog jackets than I've ever seen.
Outdoors, the May sun is still almost merciful.
The warm Atlantic would have us in for a bath,
but the jellyfish got there first.

If you go out walking in the pines, best
to move thoughtfully now, for the snakes,
by May, have gotten themselves out of bed.
And be watchful too if you walk into town,
for there are no sidewalks along the roads
dense, as never before, with cars
rushing to either river or beach.

And at night, be most watchful of all,
for when the television is off and you walk
outdoors, your own past surprises you,
rises up from every direction,
overwhelms with its distant cries,

keen warmth and sorrow.
And you remember how armies of young men and old
once gathered not far from here and died.

Our last day in Southport we drove to the newer cemetery,
to the gravestones of two good friends, Betty and Don—
lovers on their second marriage each.
They had painted, gardened, sewn, knitted, baked,
made jokes together, and offered their pool,
year after year, to our young daughters.
Don died some years before Betty, and Betty passed
on the day our first grandchild was conceived.

And I wonder and wonder:
if I breathe in even briefly the pure oxygen
of my own unknown, can I acclimate
to some greater sky around me?

&

FORTIETH ANNIVERSARY PRAYER

This ceaseless river,
and you, lit portal, ark. Love,
make us seaworthy.

WHATEVER IS LIVING

I.

If a scent brings childhood back,
what if anything is far from us?
Jonelle and I in Colorado are barefoot
on the hot alley stones, in her big chaotic house,
in my grandmother's rock garden, amidst the lilacs.
We are running from our little sisters.
We are hidden in Jonelle's black closet
with the phosphorescent Virgin. Tomorrow,
we will build a tent house that has five rooms.
She may make me invisible with vinegar
and a hundred mint leaves.
We will burn our hair together as blood sisters.
We will dance in the mud of any thunderstorm.

And play goes on and on, summer has no walls.
Dry heat, day after day, is the forever of summer.
Whatever is living shimmers like waves
of hot air above the alley, that vein
which connects us.
And everything, everything is living.

II.

Time too has no walls,
though we do not know this.
And the desert is not far from town,
we are guests of its silence.
Time and the desert circle us, even in our play.
They penetrate our blood and limbs,
sear names and bodies into ours with living heat,
run, as we do, everywhere.

And we who are innocent of this
play on and on, holding open our screen doors
for each other many times in a day.
Which sibling should we run from?
Should we hide in the basement room
or under the low-branched pine?
What room should we move to
in my grandmother's sweet-smelling house
or in the big chaotic house? We don't know
what will next embody us,
but we'll find out, now and now.
We never stop for long, and the days are long
to make ourselves up as we go.

III.

And my grandmother is still watering her lilacs.
They change but do not die back.
The other ancestors are waiting too
in the ripening night.
Waiting beyond war, struggle, and the dusty porches
for *our* becoming.
They look out through the eyes of our children.
They have left themselves behind
and they are still who they were—both at once.

And my grandmother and the other ancestors
are handing over into our hesitant hands
the red garden hose, cracked but still good.
They do not speak in words
but their need and hope are thunder.
They are asking us, now, here,
forever and grown-up,
never to cease watering the still-living
lilacs of their own transformation.

The Singer Moving Everywhere at Will

THE SINGER MOVING EVERYWHERE AT WILL

And so, as he moves, he gathers them

> *comet's tail telling*
> *fire to dolphin*
> *ruby-gift-of-the-earth*
> *touching night-green spider*
> *mountain aspen alone*
> *trembling above all-forgotten*
> *valleys*

saying, you have waited for me,
moving everywhere at will

> *lizard lingering at the fountain*
> *mouse sheltering*
> *under purple-lantern lupine*
> *hummingbird losing herself*
> *in yellow dahlias*

saying, spark the dark path, yes
where particles of song find you

> *mouse sheds fear under the lupine*
> *dolphin trails pure joy onto the path*
> *night-green spider learns light*
> *from ruby-gift-of-the-earth*

saying, I travel ahead and behind
everywhere, here

lizard finds tongues of water
hummingbird
folded
stills herself in yellow dahlias

to find you and you,
and again, always, you

aspen knows she is not forgotten

BEFORE THIS POEM TURNED TO WORDS

Before this poem turned to words,
I raised my arms and asked the birds
if they would rise and come to greet
our newly gathered flocks and herds.

"Our day is young, the sun is new,
and many pin their hopes on you.
We've waited here so long to see
if song could really set us free."

The birds replied, "We sing alone,
but if you'll shield our blood and bone,
be shelter to our every wing,
we'll rise and tell you everything."

That said, their song began anew,
and I, now older, paused and grew.
I joined the animals on the grass.
We watched the summer, poignant, pass.

And all who listened on that field
heard their stories sound, revealed.
No day not seen, no night not known.
To each was sung his blood, her bone.

The sheep lay trembling as one.
The cows were pensive in the sun.
And all our breadcrumbs, proffered, free,
returned to us as ecstasy.

FOR MY FIFTH GRADERS MOVING ON

Seed, seed
open wide, not afraid
hello goodbye, beginning end
will end *you*, but leave, stretch, fly, bend
split open, never easy, no straight road, yet just begin
in fragrant soil, new rooms (spacious, wide)
road just ahead, the next one and the next
sprout into flower, bush, tree, and be
beginning new (not lonely), hear
through all new doors (to sing)
the one true song
that's only
yours

YOU FIREFLIES OF INSIGHT

You fireflies
 of insight innate
 bees
of illumination
carrying yellow
  all-fruit
particle to particle in
  April
    birth-crowning

    alight now you
seeming small in air and over
      lemon wild onion lavender last year's
snapdragons rosemary's storm you

    in poured light return
humming beings over
     grass and time's
splintered deck
  fountain maple mint
    camellia beyond
  the fence all

   perfect now
in moving warm in April's
   hand to toll honey

swell of plum
 cream of sound
    like cello in early morning
  garden of
your secret
   summer

INCANTATION FOR A SICK CHILD

Speak, speak, unknown one,
descent into the membrane, the seized blood,
cells with battle wings spread
over the hot, dry field,
no song spared, none:
Cool the wounds of her mouth,
allay fever, make small the carried cross
of anger, loss,
sadness in its still pool.

And voice, fire, ice,
marry in her for the melding
of flesh with newborn
vision, the walking back
into herself, lift in the bone.

Oh you, speaking, singing one,
heard one, be what is hers only,
returned, burned bright in her,
clear, clear.

THE OUTSIDER

—for Rutheda

Left behind in heaven,
locked out of the earth,
who is this that hovers
without a birth?

Walking not the mountain,
touching not the day,
deathless and desiring
formless to stay;

Never feels the swell of sleep,
never lives a season,
waiting at the borderland
of sight and reason:

All the time, outsider,
you we never know
waver, wordless, where
we dare not go.

Nothing in our daily being,
sure of what we seek,
perceives you at our shore,
trying to speak.

You amidst dimensions
aching at our side
sorrow for the depths
from which we hide.

But to listen, listen
would be to find you here,
self anterior to self,
encircled in the ear.

‌

WHAT THE GNAT SAID TO THE LIGHTBULB

—for my Students

See how I
                climb glass
to you, a
blazing
  planet, dreaming
                the sun
                is near
        and simple

I could risk all
like my brother
  moth
for you   nearness
        of my

small sun
but oh
brightness, heat
huge one, my many

legs, my wings, how they
        (like a whisper)
in you would perish
no

I am not
my brother
moth
 I love my
        flight
into   all
        large colors

and there are
        one hundred thousand
            still
(or more)
steps
        my many legs
will make
 on walls and
 windows

of this world

E. DICKINSON CONNOTES THE
MYSTERY OF PATIENCE TO ONE LIVING

Your Honeysuckle stitch forbids
Temptation—of the Sky—
Too large a Gulp it tries to take—
Descend—enough—to try

Sculpting a tiny Moment—
The clear glass, the clean
Wood of a cold Dimension—
Not only—merely—seen—

And holding fast the Netting—
That darkens over—Time—
Push to one side a Grandeur—
Obedient—to Design—

Obedient, my Friend, to speak
The Nature of Retreat—
Before again resuming
The Tapestry—complete—

Your Honeysuckle—died away—
Your Pine went on—and grew—
What Saturday does not destroy
What Friday thought—it knew—

The Known—a perfect obstacle—
The True—a stolid Wall—
But Follicle—of urgency—
A Shimmering—a Call—
Burst open to the New—

STREET LITTER IN A SPRING OF RAIN

—to Gerard Manley Hopkins

You drift-dance shreds, white plastic ghosts lighting
on random corners, rotten rind and core
of dead fruit tossed onto streets by lost hands;
you torn paper, ripped leaves flown, blown
in the air wide-open, past locked houses in grey
wet skies of April—you random ones, not rare:

Are you too, like us, the strange lives lived
skimming earth in air, praying to perfect and take back
the untorn pieces of yourselves, not shorn of core,
dropped blindly away, splintered?
Even you blown ones, once tree, fruit, earth's ancient
fauna, flora—you too stop atop and against
walls, bodies greater than your own.
Which know your words torn away.
Which burn what has stayed for true warmth.

And if they cast you into the sea
that is waiting for you, for me, all wanderers
in an unfinished chasm, we will meet
each other alive, changed,
frayed, unafraid,
beyond hearing or sight.
Brought new out of sand, brought new
out of the fecund mud born
when the hard rains fall and fall.

SPELL SONG FOR THE DAY
OF THE DEAD

Hunter, hunter, find your mark
in the wide, illumined dark.
Hunted fall and prey will cry.
Transfigured into air we die.

All beneath death, the earth.
All beneath bells, the will of fall:
the skimming of death, the shaken to earth,
scrim of bare branch and taken leaf
in the large mouth of a mother making us
yearn for arms to take us, telling
our years like bells, into the well we await.

Oh well of told things made clear
to heart's ear, taught to the listening child
caught by life's near, straggling motions;
and the unclear, chaotic mirror unfolded,
unfurled wide, narrowed to one side
before broken down, drifting sharp before
the rung harp of winter: all goes into
the bone-blood, and flood of weeping and laughing
spreads like a river lapping
the living and dead as one.

Lost the summit, lost the mine
where the ore's elixirs shine.
We are hungry: Who will fill
our bodies with his winter will?
Ring, ring, all will ring.
Darts of the sun, arrows of moon:
target the heart and reach us soon.

POWER OUTAGE

So still, from hours of wind out of control—
this dark, this page with secrets, answering
a prayerless night. Its pen moves through our rubble.
Makes restless eyes rest, perceive the cycling
of birth and death, stay unafraid to meet
such perfect black, the void of their completion.
Makes ears welcome an enforced retreat
into the forests of loss, attrition,
meet the soundlessness that is their mother.
Who are we now, stopped, stark, as November
circles in her dance? Here, while another
minute of a tale we won't remember
dawns, turns, moves this long dark to toll
return, unfathomed, into the soul.

ENIGMAS ON A MORNING IN JUNE

What stream runs deeper than birth?
What question have we forgotten to ask?
Is there more than one true home?
What is the undone task?

Who walks in our garden without us?
What do snow-masked mountains hide?
Where is silence born in the body?
Where does patience reside?

What closure narrowed the vision?
What lock keeps out the new?
Who closed the door on the treasure?
Whose tongue made chyme from the new?

Deeper than birth runs the question.
Patience, the task undone.
The Visitor waits in the garden
Where creeks of snow-melt run.

The lock was broken by snow-melt.
The fecund treasure grew.
The narrows—streams of the forgotten—
Perceived, ran clear and new.

The intimate gate made open,
The intimate ground made soft:
Illumine the whorls of the ear
Where home resounds, aloft.

OF PARABLE AND FLIGHT
(AN ANCIENT SONG)

I once fell into a world so small
it could not hold the light at all
   but shrunk my half-formed soul
and crowded out each living thing
that might have turned to speak or sing
   and burst me from the whole.

The garden birds were laughing, sweet,
the fountain poured, but in retreat
   I watched from down below.
And spring returned, my children grew,
yet chained to what I thought I knew,
   I could not stay or go.

The limbo of eternity,
stranded where no friend could be,
   afraid to liquefy
and lose my caterpillar sight,
familiar home, the well-lit night—
   to these I could not die;

Nor shed, abandon by the road
endeavor as unwieldy load
   and welcome chrysalis,
the sheer unknown of latent cells,
the embryonic wings and bells—
   I could not leap to this.

One stairway stopped. Above, beyond:
another. And the chasm yawned
  before my shaking feet.
I stepped back down, walked back indoors,
immersed myself in daily chores,
  made light of my defeat.

Until the year one butterfly
airborne, flew close and uttered, "Try.
  Receive yourself in flight."
I'd aged to grief, sobriety,
the chrysalis lay there for me,
  staircases spanned the night.

And plumbing the eye of that unknown
which out of every object shone,
  and piercing the heart of sound,
I glimpsed the course of daily needs
and burned for that whose timeless seeds
  could penetrate my ground;

While night and day my garden's scent
muted the weathers' argument
  with vivid vapors, crying,
"It's yours to read, this tender book.
But in your trembling overlook,
  keep close the art of dying."

And every fear at last seemed
particle of the dead and dreamed;
  true dying, always new.
What precious time had brought to birth
now shed itself upon the earth,
  now moving, moistened—flew.

IN JOY THE CHILD ALONE

Let darkness bloom
chrysanthemums
purple and yellow
in the room

my heart has made,
my heart has built
out of the glass
of time and silt.

This is the room
that has no key,
unfinished,
where a mystery

leads in the night.
It is the call
of petals
into which I fall.

These flowers are
a spring unknown.
Night is their provenance,
mind their sun,

and I am the child
whose lap is full,
whose chamber opens
on whole worlds.

I will retrieve
each sun and moon,
let each and all
suffuse my room,

and no one will search
to find me here
where I am alone
with all things near.

INDIAN SUMMER
(REMEMBRANCE)

1)

Ripe world in tawny harvest,
ripe truth in autumn's oak,
we've followed hope to cities
where joy is laced with smoke.

Somewhere there heals in hidden
woods, some ancient trust
once planted in joy's children
but harvested in rust.

Oh heart's forgotten journey,
oh answer from a stream
forgotten: mend this honey.
To our dying leaves, send wings.

This quest—a burnished orchard
still infinite, but dark,
but falling—be our remembering,
in gratitude and ache.

And courage by creekside, breathe
into soul's sad mountain
maple's honor and wisdom's grass.
Till this long birthing pass.

2)

Leaves drop down to the infinite.
Memories circle us, calling.
Fears fall but we send
daughters into time's wind.
What lamplight staves off winter?
Night and time are both falling.
The amber earth forgets nothing.
Memory is always calling.

3)

Now it grows late, late.
We begin to forget
what once we could trust
in orchard, oak, and wing,
long day's slow glowing.

The overcrowded city of the soul
is glutted now, knows neither grass
nor the infinite call
of children on a journey.
It amasses, yet grows small.

Will its long-gathered truth fall to rust,
to the unhealed ache and dark
creek of a broken quest?
Heart turn to smoke,
its harvest lost?

Or, in reflection, seal
dry wood to the green,
or to one still unknown, unseen,
even more real
than summer? Or meet

despair with the slow-growing scent
of moistening mulch, unexpectedly sweet,
after leaves have dropped from the maple.
Unexpectedly gleaning what is supple—
though it is not possible to retreat.

4)

And in this browning,
deepening down,
to play
silence
like a flute
listen
to the way
this leaf falls, and that

Domestic Sequence
(*A Calendar*)

DOMESTIC SEQUENCE
(A CALENDAR)

1,2

Winter's bare banches.
Harder and harder to hide
from all my neighbors.

Morning again. Ice.
This cold is not a dream. Does
my lemon tree live?

3, 4

From dark into day
I sat. And before each tree,
first, its silhouette.

Why not read haiku
to my ancient cat? She so
quietly listens.

5, 6

Little impatiens,
droop. It's winter. Why pride
yourself on beauty?

Who to thank? Our huge
avocado tree planted
herself. Didn't budge.

7, 8

the state of man, gleaned on a shopping trip

Shock, pain, disbelief!
That half-wanted dress was gone
when I went back for it.

Beloved, forgive
my hunger of last night.
I want too much—and now.

9, 10

anniversary of the death of one
who died on Valentine's Day

You left for new worlds.
Our grief. . .and that of all who
sleep alone this night.

If mind, at its best,
is mirror, then what is this
undulating world?

11, 12

Old Robert, widowed,
nearly blind, gropes with his hands
our path of houses.

Give it up! Why hope?
You will never glimpse the sky
from this dark hallway.

13, 14

hearing one loved was mortally ill

Sorrow in mid-May.
Lupine rampant. The sudden
cold petals of tears.

Hidden tears, easy
to wash away in the bath,
like spring rains return.

15, 16

In summer, insight.
In fall and winter, study.
Spring? Bittersweetness.

our annual mockingbird and my friend,
a fine soprano

All that June night long,
wooing he sang, as Ann Mia
gave birth to a son.

17, 18

Summer fog again.
Silence. Grey sidewalks, skies.
As below, above.

Sea-fog mutes July.
But our summer mockingbird
sings all night long.

19, 20

Why, when my girls were
grown, did you stop coming, you
tireless mockingbird?

And even if you answer
with silence, my friend,
death is no excuse!

21, 22, 23, 24, 25, 26

in October 2000, our next door neighbor was
killed by her boyfriend with her children present

W ords on a page, screen.
Your young son sitting on our
step that night. Two worlds.

Do ghosts take the form
of flowers? The camellia
above where Claire died.

Window cat next door.
We make love in the light room
above where Claire died.

Claire, the mockingbird,
my girls, the fence cat, all gone
for now. *Fear? Wonder?*

Pulling the curtains back.
So much more, Claire, than our
beginning or end.

what Miriam told me a year after Daddy died

The woman opened
her cloak. A tiny baby.
What's his name? "Owen."

27, 28

*I dreamed the Devil sat with us
around our kitchen table*

"You might say," he said,
"I'm something about 'doing'."
He crossed his legs, laughed.

Nothing in the dream
but our lemon tree, until
a voice said, "*See it.*"

29, 30, 31

What is the poem?
Trace, echo, storm, scent? A sound
comes out of the hand.

What is the poem?
A grey bird descends, alights,
carrying the sky.

Whatever cannot
be said: that is what is called,
that is the poem.

32

Is it you? Your son?
And did you hear these poems?
Mockingbird is back!

Occasional Crones, Elves
and M.F.K. Goofrock

THE CRONE ASCENDING

—for Lori on her 50th Birthday

There was an old lady named Lolly
Who cast aside all youthful folly.
    The only thing was
    You couldn't tell 'cause
She still looked infernally jolly!

"Pray, what is your secret?" we queried.
"Why is it you never look wearied?"
    But Lolly just winked,
    Grinned, twinkled and blinked,
Till the rest of us poor souls felt bleuried.

She said, "A crone's secrets are legion,
And hail out of many a region.
    If I tell you, you'll steal 'em,
    Or sell 'em or deal 'em,
So why should I go and reveal 'em?!"

"O Lolly, we love you!" we said.
"Lie down in your soft feather bed.
    Your two feet we'll rub,
    Give you champagne and tub,
If the secrets of Cronehood you'll shed."

"I'm sold!" Lolly said, "I acknowledge
It started last century in college
    With daft predilections
    For making predictions
And for that we need never apolig.!"

"One Feb. 29 with libation
Despite Jane Stan*ford's* limitation,
    We all in our glory,
    Mary-Linda-Claude-Lori,
Began with bizarre inspiration

"To predict which of us would be kissed
In the quad, and who would be missed.
    Who'd travel or work,
    Break up with a jerk,
And thus began list after list!"

"Each year we would meet and proclaim
Which one would win dubious fame.
    Who'd marry a surgeon
    And who'd stay a virgin
Was parcel and pith of our game!"

"And now that I'm old and hot-flashing
When other old ladies are crashing,
    All I have to do
    If I start to get blue
Is turn my old brain to rehashing

"The four of us spewing out fiction
And a *wee* bit o'truth in prediction.
    My troubles all wither
    Remembering our dither,
And I laugh at all life's contradiction!"

"And so, let me sing like a lark,
Defying both shadow and shark.
    With love I am showered
    And always empowered
To hit each high note on the Mark!"

And now, our dear Lolly, we greet you
As 50-plus years come to meet you.
    May birthday dreams stay
    To come true every day,
So nothing in life can defeat you!

ELF SONG
(*Pick Your Year!*)

Hail friends and family, young and old,
We greet you from the Elfin fold!
In case you thought that we're kaput,
Well, let's just say that point is *moot*!
Yes, we're around, we're unabated.
You might could say that we're UPDATED!
No more to don a cap or tight,
We've metamorphed—we're made of light!
Zip! Zap! 'tween earth and heaven,
We're here and working 24/7.
We hear a sigh, a groan, a yelp,
And *zoom*! in a flash, we're there to help.
We'll send an epiphany, melt that pout.
If there's a problem we'll work it out!
But stay alert, 'cause you can't see us.
(We're quieter than a newborn Prius!)

So raise your glass, your cookie, your mug,
Whether driving a freeway, fixing a rug,
Nabbing a steelhead, feeding a kitty,
Planting a veggie, writing a ditty,
Checking your email, playing Sudoko,
Texting your sister, sipping your cocoa,
Reading a mystery, shopping at TJ's,
Dressin' up nice, puttin' on PJ's,

Walking your dog, checking her barking,
Calling a friend, looking for parking,
Lying in bed or multi-tasking:
HEAR OUR SONG—that's all we're asking!
Light that menorah, trim that tree,
But don't believe everything you see!
And whether you clink with brew or mojito,
And whether you feast on bird or burrito,
Here's joy, health, love and every reason
To celebrate and toast the season!
　　　HAPPIEST HOLIDAYS TO ALL!!

THE LOVE SONG OF M.F.K. GOOFROCK

—for Rue and her fellow Libran, T.S. Eliot, on her 50th birthday, and
in honor of shared first adventures at a country retreat center

Let us go then, we and Rue
When the evening is laid out like a roll of Su–
Shi sliced and juicy on the table:
Let us walk, Crones all, while we are able
Through half-deserted cabins and motel rooms,
With pillow case and bedspread and with paint;
Walk past friends cooking, sweeping, and in maint-
Enance, and give our nod to gardening,
Now, while our arteries are not yet hardening.
Oh, do not say, "Why do it?" or "I blew it."
It's time to muddle through it. . .

> *On the shelves, the Mouselings climb and putter*
> *Dreaming of cracker crumbs and peanut butter.*

And indeed there will be time,
Time to wash and time to fold
One hundred towels,
Time to soothe an ancient Corgi's growls.
There will be time, there will be time
To spruce up yet another room,
And over unbrought bedding sometimes fume!
Time to meet and plan and make a list,
And time in the night recalling things you missed.
Time to sing, talk and wax terse,
And time for all decisions and revisions
Which a Libran in a moment can reverse!

> *And now and then, the Raccoon on all fours*
> *Says, "Won't someone crack the kitchen doors?"*

And we have known them all, known the beasts:
Known Indigo and Ollie and Kabir,
Patted this furry head and scratched that ear.
And yes, yes, we have shared our feasts
With Mouse and Raven, Ant and Fly, and Deer.
Of any creature, Rue may have her choice.
Oh, Crones, rejoice!

I should have been a pair of broken vacuums
Screeching across the floor in clouds of dust. . .

And would it have been worth it after all,
Would it have been worthwhile,
After the many meals and washing dishes,
Between the hot cups and the paper towels,
Among the votives, knives and hotel pans,
If one Mouse, nibbling a plastic bag
And smothering a smile, should say,
"That was not what I meant to eat,
That was not it at all."

Yes, we must mew and howl, oh Kitten, Dogs,
And squeak, oh Mouse, and croak, you pond of Frogs.
(They will say, "She grows bold. . .she grows bold. . .
How her life is getting bigger.")

And we have heard the Mermaids sing away
To Rue on this her fiftieth birthday,
Wishing her well o'er redwood, creek and Bay,
Wishing her travel, art and good *feng shui*,
Wishing her beauty, truth and money flowing,
Time galore and happy Indigo-ing. . .

And so we linger at our tables eating
Sushi, joyous birthday words repeating,
And wish Rue well at 50, now and here,
Till Beasts and Mermaids join us, and we cheer!

Approach to Magic

FREE TO GO

Before the entangled visitor loses his way
even more in the maze of roses, his sky-blue hat
bobbing above them all, we should alert him
to the possibility of loss. He could lose everything
to the rose-beings who require lost visitors
for purposes of fertilization. That anonymous man
(if man he is) has never known himself
to guard against the onslaught of so forceful
a beauty. Too late. He is taken as sacrifice,
a muted butterfly. He is dismembered,
even as we speak, into a thousand more
waving roses.

It is best to know what garden one wanders into,
though such tenuous knowledge cannot always
be given in advance. Was he married,
leaving children, a wife, friends? No, the roses
knew he was free to go. This was in fact needed
for his further growth. Indeed, it was said
that after all the other pieces of himself
were gone, subsumed into roses,
and only his face remained,
he was smiling.

FORBIDDEN PERFUME

—for my Mother

The flower says to the child,
"For you, I never sank into the earth.
For you, becoming fragrance,
I was knowledge moving on the wind.
I was perfection."

The child says,
"It was a beautiful blue bottle,
smaller than my hand.
I could not hide when it broke;
the forbidden perfume
lost itself in the room, revealing all."

The right hand says,
"The startled water and blood
spiraled down the sink to a river
beyond reach of any childhood.
But the mother was not angry,
for her child was seeking a Fragrance."

The scar says,
"I became the divide
between right and left.
I reveal that the side of the body
most eagerly touched is as easily injured."

The scar goes on:
"You age, but I remain.
For you, I am always the call into that
which climbs, unbottled, onto the sky.
What is blood lost for a fragrance?
Child, never forget what I am."

AFTER GRIEF

My friend who had lost her husband
visited her sister-in-law in Florida,
stood before a wall at NASA,
stood there, waited and waited.
Stood even longer.
Till she knew in her bones,
and maybe even in her blood,
what light-years are.

❧

INSCRIPTION NEAR THE GATE OF THE LABYRINTH

Would you see and see again an alternate ending?
Not to know yourself is the only error.
Fragments of a wounded planet, winding
their way back home, reside in every mirror.

IMPERISHABLE THREADS OF HEAVEN

We get onto the bus in Chinatown.
He is two seats away from us, the strange
old Asian man—ragged, whiskered, curved nails
white with fungus, shock-blue tennis shoes
huge on his feet, no socks.
Yet his cheeks are surprisingly ruddy,
and I realize this old man is around my age.

Now he begins to sing.

He is serenading my young granddaughter.
It is a children's song I half-recognize,
loudest on the refrain, again and again:
Don't be afraid. Then he moves to poetry,
A Garden of Verses, the one stanza I know
to say to her, always at the park:
"*How do you like to go up in a swing. . .*"
But he knows the second verse we don't.
His voice grows, it is resonant, finer,
clearer with every line. It is all for us,
and glorious. Then he is quiet.
A young woman gets on, sits between us.
The old man gets off a few blocks later.

Imperishable threads of heaven
meet in the eyes and ears,
twine into the gold, incorruptible,
any true alchemist would give his life for.

PATIENCE CONNOTING HERSELF AS A NEW DIMENSION

"Time, space, and patience are those channels through which man as a finite mind may become aware of the infinite." —Edgar Cayce

Say stay
to lay my ferment
    living foam
 against dark rush
thinned
 entropy of speed
massed shards of shards shaken
 the already dying, died

    oh stay, yes,
I am here, yes, not far
    stirred and stirring
hand in an open bowl, decanted
 wine of time and space, breath
of leaves and waves
    sightless mole's sting
      of light
    tender rain

 and I more
to you, more deep
than tissue, blood, cell,

more of moving, living lymph
 to rack of want, pain
I your infusion, true
   tale's telling
   oh

undiminished craftsman,
           say
       stay now and now
to me, arc, replenishing
       stream to and with and from
       all, the moment's
summoning, full
       unfolding

WHILE WATCHING PASSERSBY IN LATE AFTERNOON RAIN

For a moment, you are stunned into watchfulness:
a congealing, an open door where
these before you in the rain, like the sound-thought
of a violin, the gesture of a hand,
all remind you (who would always travel home)
of the weather of return.

No scent, but even more fleeting,
the memory of a scent. And memory's wings
opened briefly. Not narrow flat ground
but a staircase, spiraling up and down, on which
you and these others are always moving.
The help great, even if hidden, but the stakes
higher than you ever knew.

Traveler, do not hesitate to leave behind
any precious stones you were intent on gathering.
Your small mind gapes, and cannot fathom its smallness;
your great mind still keeps secret its timeless lake.
Better, empty-handed, to go on looking—
open-eyed, amidst others, in day's darkening—
for that which remembered you in the beginning.

OF EMPTINESS: A FIRST CONTEMPLATION

"Form is emptiness, emptiness is form. Form is not other than empti-
ness; emptiness is not other than form." —Buddhist Heart Sutra

An empty cup connotes the tea,
the hand, another hand.
The yellow chamber in the flower,
a scented land.

Must something happen? Yes, we wait
in empty space for that. Yet
perhaps a house retrieves itself
the hour we move out.

Taste emptiness? Let it play
in quiet on the page, the new
blank yellow notebook? In the mind
before the infant day?

Assent to it? Uncloseted
expanse, an endless steppe
travelled in staying still?

Oh beginner, now
stand, be, where
knowingly you breathe
unanswered air.

APPROACH TO MAGIC

You are beginning to become unknown to yourself,
a winter to yourself. Inarticulate. You have grown,
and still grow, slow to yourself, unseen, unlit.
There are precious stalagtites in your airless secret home.
They have formed over time so measureless
that you tune yourself to the unseen, only that.
Yet you live amidst houses, humans, trees, streets. . .

You are not young.
Each day, you make the bed, drink tea, go out,
come back, hang up your coat anew.
You are exposed to the elements even indoors,
as you (and all others) are meant to be a bare branch.
The weather changes each hour, and your weaknesses
have rooted, the maze of them assails you, repeats,
is part of your nerves, your blood.
You have lost all facile hope.

But pressed into need, you are freed
of both your path and your past. You must be
clutched by nothing. It is beyond dusk now,
it is dark, and you are pressed into need,
a work, a threshold.
There is no way back,
no choice but to turn and return
to the winter crystal of your being.
Hold it as you can. Perhaps
encounter magic.

A ROSE STANDS GUARD OVER THE SOUL

—for Kristine

A rose stands guard over the soul,
a resolute perfume,
its petals close in curtaining
the secret birthing room.

Chameleon yellows, mauve and pink,
the salmons and the white,
shelter by turns a newness
that first unfurls by night.

Suffer the rose at your window,
suffer it at your door.
That thorn, that knife upheld in love,
comes faithful, calm, pure.

Chameleon beauty magnifies
the fruit, and fans the blaze
your crucible ignites to be
the crimsoning of days.

What price the birthing room, the knife,
the fruitless and the fruit,
if struggling embryo were not
sublimity and root?

HOMEOPATHY

Belladonna, hellstone
stop the fever in the bone

> *what the mother and father hated*
> *foundling left for lost, child*
> *of the locked garden*

strychnine, venom, toxic leaf
unravel pain and grief

> *born blind, mineral, mold*
> *the willing germ, the eager virus*

honey bee, bird's wing
arsenic, acid, flint, root
strange or hated thing dilute

> *how you walk, talk, turn in your bed*
> *your precise outcry calls to its echo*

make them small, and smaller still,
minute, until the dreaded, odd,
conjoin the cells of God

> *and sight beyond suffering pries itself loose*
> *poison to light, and light to the stinging stone*
> *transformed, reverberant in blood and nerve,*

and what you are, heard, arises new
> *from the myriad and old*
> *profound and most*
> *healed wound*

THIS FURNACE CANNOT BURN

This furnace cannot burn
alchemically to grace
without
high heat and willing fuel.

Prepare the cord to break,
the severing to proceed
where none dare watch,
so great the need
for final freedom.

This vision momentary,
this vascular consuming,
this sobering, this reckoning of space
between advance, retreat:

And so to live, to leave
phosphoric in defeat.

WEEKEND AWAY

Flew back to Portland a month after Nora's bat mitzvah.
Your brother, luminous and sad, had taken his life.
You wanted to drive us—Nora and me—
to the Oregon beach you'd loved in childhood.
It had been only a month, but your face was thinner,
and from trouble, even beyond Randy's disappearance,
the timbre of your voice had altered.

Now at the Eagleton beach, it had just stopped raining.
A wind came up, sudden, strangely ferocious.
It pushed the three of us forward, lifted the sand,
formed it in ghostlike sheets, primeval fins,
hundreds of them, moving all around us.
The wind was a living thing split open.

Then Nora threw down a small blue ball.
It went forward in the wind, didn't lurch or swerve.
It rolled on in the fury, sure of itself, not quite
straight but slowly finding, making its path.
Deviating only as a thin stream twists
ahead in a familiar creek bed. As a toddler
shakes on her feet but makes the next step.

We followed the ball half a mile or so.
We had no choice. Nora finally ran forward,
picked it up. The wind died back after that.
We left the beach, walked back to our inn.

Nora slept in next morning, Sunday,
but we two went early to the beach—
to that new silence, April sun.
Sea-grass and sand were glowing,
clamshells and sand dollars everywhere.

What came as you walked were the words, at last,
of a sermon for Randy you might offer many people.
What came my way was a sand dollar marred
by a dark, three-sided hole. It seemed worth keeping.
It showed through to another side of things.

Flew back home that afternoon, a short flight.
Tried to watch, really catch, the transitions:
how clouds changed as we rose,
where the Trinity River began, how Mt. Shasta
turned to hills, and hills became vineyards and farms
turning to cities, and how the grey shipyards of Oakland,
close under our plane, changed again,
becoming the dear asphalt we touched.

But it was impossible. That large movement was both
too gradual and too quick. And I wondered how Change
puts sand in our eyes always. Covers her tracks
as she works around and in us.

Then I noticed, suddenly and with surprise,
I had lost my fear of flying.

ONLY BY THIS SHALL WE BE KNOWN

"Anonymity is the prerequisite for the entrance into heaven."
—*Ananda Coomaraswamy*

Pressed knowingly into sand, a shape
that won't live out the night,
transparency we wear and are,
clear wool wound tight;
this shell of skin, and wondering
what or who falls
into form as raw insight:
oh, in what freedom find
such clamshell hope, the unnamed
leaves' delight,
the work of winds.
As a woman singing
to her child alone by night,
or beads that onto willing
strings some god
may yet invite.

IRELAND JOURNAL

1) *At the summer solstice, after Carrowmore*

The stones are again alone. Perhaps
breeze- and rain-blown in this briefest night.
It is midsummer's clarion call, with dusk
near midnight, dawn at four.
And now, there, even if not yet dark,
it is night. And now, this night's brief vigil
blows breath of buttercup, chrysanthemum,
grass, red clover over the stones.

And the stones are alive.
At night after travelers leave, while cows sleep,
while crows and gulls are still, the stones
are alive in their locked cypher.
Alive in the night and alone.

We flew home late last week.
There was no rain the week we saw the stones.
Our Sligo cabby said, "They're praying for you,
back home, to get such weather."
We stayed for hours.

There are no words for the stones, yet
there is one poem in the body for every stone.
And a poem in the body for each
circle or chamber near trimmed grass,
clear paths. And one for each
whose circle breaks. And one for each
in wilder grass, uncut, behind
the wooden fence we climbed.
And poems for those half-buried, hidden, great.
One poem or a hundred.

Each stone tells what it can.
Together they tell what they can.
We let them say what they could
in rude translation without words.
Penetrating past these ears and eyes
glutted with years, and into
the one hearth of the heart—
an empty hearth where every unformed word
can burn there, simply.

It is as if we ourselves are stone-lit rooms,
too long closed, now opened.
We were too inward, never having heard
our own vast reverberations.
But after the stones, even if briefly,
we echo fire, simply.

%

We sat a long time on the stones.
We stood before the stones as living bodies,
bodies joined with the many
who have sat, walked, lived, died
within these circles, or in the tabled dark.

We were seeking beyond ourselves to meet ourselves.
We were and are the temporal, unrooted, unnoted,
but also the travelers and the touched.
We came to see and were instead the watched.

%

We listened. As back home, we listen now.
The still tableaux will stay, will teach,
the cells of stone remain while we move on—
brief day into long night. But time perhaps

will shift as we wind onward.
We'll follow switchbacks back. We'll let
what cannot die flame willingly in grass.
And like the stones, we'll live
our daily cypher,
moving against all odds to meet
unfinished covenants.
We'll walk our maze and navigate
the knot, so intricate, of immortality,
form into new form bent.

And though the city of stone will stay,
we'll go where we are sent.

2) *Holy Well*

   The wildflower wind is blowing centuries back. It brings us to
the small sign unexpectedly seen in the hills above Killarney. We
follow where it points, we slip behind a cattle gate beyond warm fields.
Here is a shroud of old woods, and here, not far away, an oak marked
by the white paint of a simple cross. At its base, a concrete bowl.

   Is this it? Is this the holy well? A "seep" murky, mere inches
deep, encircled with rocks by long dead hands? But this is no wishing
well, no clear uprising to the air. It is no firm vision or slaked thirst.
Instead, as we stand above it, something else gathers, hovering here.
It is some isolated sorrow. It is pain streaming mid-air. It is something
old as the well, as seeping water from the almost closed earth—the
water which rises a little, stays.

   Now, suddenly, we are no longer tourists. To the lesions of hunger,
desperation, violent hidden acts, we stand open, we do not move.
And this unseen is not ours to skim, to answer lightly, but to enter.
We must submerge ourselves in witness. Bear need in the shade of
witness. Bear ultimate prayer and death.

We are not strangers now, not would-be pilgrims at a holy seep, hoping for new light. We fall instead into time's bed, a spiral moving backward and ahead all at once. Is this what remains of some tale of "others"? Of others' losses or their exultations? Of others' past and passing?

"Who are these others?" asks the wise man. And the answer, like the seep, rises, though still murky. Pulses into our wrists, our throats, our limbs, now and long after. To be heard. To be seen. Not stopping. And staying, staying.

3) *At Galway Bus Station*

In the world's fastest-growing atheist nation (so we've been told), we wait for the bus on Saturday. Sweat and wait with many in this strange heat; turn, in our wait, to our neighbors.

The white-haired woman from Knock wears an enameled Virgin around her neck. She is traveling home and describes the apparition of Her that thousands will honor this weekend in Knock. Fervent and serene, she has no home but Knock. She invites us to get off the bus before Sligo, at Knock. We will share in the shrine she loves.

Behind her, the young man from Derry tells of meeting two Jesuits, young aspirants, even now on a three-week walk from Derry to Dublin. They carry no cell phones or money. Can't reveal who they are until offered shelter or food. The test of faith unremitting. Walking, walking even now.

Finally the bus arrives, and passengers of every race, both tourists and Irish, board as we do. The human flurry dies with all sound but the bus motor. And now, as so often in Ireland, between and behind the undulant waves of traffic, the crush of crowds, the curl of speech, we enter a silence that is bottomless.

4) *At Newgrange*

The young Asian woman is alone on a bench near the barns, near the old great tomb. It is the tour's lunch hour, she is playing an Irish harp. It is soft song unexpected under overcast skies.

She says she's from Japan and always dreamed of playing, in Ireland, an Irish harp. She says that as a child she read every Irish story she could find. She dreamed as a child by night that she was stolen by fairies. Was surprised, by morning, that she wasn't.

I tell her I too have longed so long to be here. And here we are.

She is young. She is the wondering that comes from afar. She is the traveler from afar, she awaits what falls from her fingers like seeds of light. She is taking back her gifts into the future. She is the wondering that has no death. And she is the preparation, the steeling, for a time, finally, when what is *needed* becomes the *revealed*.

5) *Glendalough (after Clara and Greg's Wedding)*

Late winter light runs pink and violet
between rains, with a white mist through
the hills beyond the lake, a delicate
half-spring, bridelike in the glen. Hue
of gorse, new blossoms, or the soul's keening
skyward. Below, our feet go to sharp
stone, steep path, our ears to the verdant meaning
that might have fallen out of Kevin's harp.
A black goat forages behind us on
the hill; a tiny bird, its bright orange breast
close to us, brazen, fears not the human,
makes of our shortbread her sublimest feast.

The old church is long gone. But the round tower
stays, witness to devotion, destruction.
Perhaps locks sorrow in its stones.
It is a simple pilgrimage we make,
to flicker here, so brief in this brief hour
amidst young joggers, tourists, buried bones
of the dead. While the flush stream joins the lake.

What else remains? Strands of meditation,
sparks in the overlook of Kevin's Cell
and Bed? Or inviolate song, a timeless heat
around the oaks and heather, an unseen bell
waiting to be heard? And what is prayer
now but tirelessness, a pause to meet
what hovers in changing light. Ineffable.
Replete. New. Fanned in cold air.

Everything about Departure

EVERYTHING ABOUT DEPARTURE
(*Page from a Personal Herbal*)

You came to California at seven and have lived with sorrel ever since. You know it never really goes away. Good for rashes, bad for gout, it makes your winter garden green. Sorrel's yellow flowers come in February, signaling spring. It grows from either root or rhizome, which means you pull up many of the thin stems (and in winter there are thousands), but many more keep tiny packets of life underground, untouched.

You enjoy sorrel in your yard awhile, enjoy its green and yellow all through chilly March. But on a warm day in April, you take out all the sorrel you can. You remember how it loves the cool damp air you came into, leaving Colorado. You remember its sour flowers in childhood forts, as salad or spikey lemonade. You remember its perseverance and how it is hated by serious gardeners. You remember it was a winter meadow, and will be once more. It will begin again small in July's cool fogs. Only strong poison can kill it.

You never knew what a rhizome meant till you tried to weed a whole yard of sorrel. Sorrel roots are claimed with ease, but not their rhizomes. This calls up for you, at 51, the burning question of darkness. Do human beings have rhizomes too? If not, can they be grown? Could you keep a small packet of life underground, in whatever world you found yourself? Wouldn't you then know everything about departure, and how, like the sorrel rhizome, to be always at home?

HER OLD AGE

After the paroxysm last November when Sadie
tore on her four legs in terror and seeming
pain along the living room windows and walls,
she never again walked to greet us at the door,
or answered to her name, or turned her head
when we clapped at her ears. And forgot
what her scratching post meant.
And talks to us often now, as never before,
meowing for all, maybe even herself, to hear.
And lies so close now (and stays and stays)
that we cannot forget we are her home. And home
is what must carry her into the distance,
nearer each day, that remembers her
as its own, a daughter.

AFTER KATRINA

In a moment she is ours too.
We fall and cannot feed our own.
We cannot find the deeper home
beneath cities of storm, ruins over water.
So desolate, the rivers newly formed
before the earth takes back her own,
that the life they carry is carrion.
We are torn apart by a white, screaming sky.
We cannot replace the unstanched blood
lost in weeping
for the cataclysm of the heart.

What vastness summons us to break?
What rage racks our living, streaming song
dying in broad daylight?
We wait, suspended, breathing.
Wait for invisible strands
of mercy, even as we fall through the tears
in the broken net of our humanness.

—August 2005

EDUCATION AND PRAYER

For several weeks I've walked more quietly
through my hall, my house, for once
knowing my two feet on the floor.
Not to be startled by the mouse
who is living near my green dresser
is more important in middle age
than ever before, having occasionally
earned the right, one hopes,
not to fear small things.

Down the street, my neighbor mourns her husband,
dead of a heart attack just last week.
How hard and short that one word is,
how rich the worlds that enfold it.
I heard her voice on the phone, but all morning
could not meet such depth.

Can I earn the right to fear big things?
To walk more quietly on the grass,
down the sidewalk, through the park;
step quietly onto the bus, seeing others?
Letting the hope and fear of transformation,
like the true fear of God, expand,
shake my depths, loosen the tightest buds?
Break me open despite myself?

Until one day I learn
to ask not that I live but that I *be*,
having met the one who is inmost
and fears nothing.

SOMEBODY ELSE'S LIFE

Yes, the foul smell of the rat
who died on our heating ducts, its corpse
irretrievable, will be with us
for several weeks. But aside from the memory
of sounds at our heat vents
for months, it may be the only way
to be reminded fully
of somebody else's life.

COME NOVEMBER

"Who will leave?" I ask myself, come November.
And our old friend, who had always searched for God,
passed away the other evening.
Dying for many months, he let the cancer come,
do its work, so that he could do his.
Drank coffee with a friend each morning
till just before he died, even did his own laundry.
Slept one day, his last, in a hospital bed.
Was loved and revered by many.

Heavy fog lay all along the coast last week.
Hours before Warren died, I drove into such fog
south of Half Moon Bay that I lost
those ahead of and behind me.
Turned off onto a detour that spilled
within minutes into sunlight, bucolic woods.
Welcomed the newly paved road.
So little time and change of sky between the two.
This life is a gift, a mortal struggle.

Now that November wanes, it seems right
to light a candle during the day, so that there is fire
while writing and cleaning, fire for cooking,
washing the dishes, for the simplest things.
And we lit many candles the other night
as we thought about our friend, and Bill asked,
"What is there to want now?" Inferring for me:
in the time we have left, both mortal struggle and gift.

I said, impractically enough
(but say it again so I won't forget),
"Impartiality. Real faith, hope and love.
A search so luminous it fills the cells.
To die like Warren."

🙚

MOTHER OF SURRENDER

Mother of surrender,
if I am melted, where will I go?
Onto lichen in the storm,
into pieces of spun moss?
Vaporize to thin light,
darken asphalt as a passing shadow?
Will I move through any small opening
of emergence or descent?
And if I spill on the floor,
rendered and ashine,
won't "Claudia," superfluous,
slip and fall?

THE POET'S SILENCE

*"I have offended God and mankind because my work did not have
the quality it should have had." —Leonardo DaVinci on his deathbed*

Unable to speak, as though an imploding wind
leaves him not desolate but stopped, stripped, numb.
So far from incantation that the hidden well
which is his to guard is as though he is away.
Lit by fluorescent light, it does not reflect the sky.

To whom would he speak, and why?
He could tell of forgotten marvels, but who would care?
Instead, in seclusion, he makes a year's journey
through his own city. Walks day after day in full light,
when all would seem clear, often passing on foot
the charged places of his youth.

Each morning, he asks how to hold
the disparate and the whole, how to honor
what is given in good faith by his life,
while shedding the no longer needed.

He knows that sooner or later his search
will end in lines of force beyond all words,
though not beyond sound. He is still so far
from what is near. And willingly he suffers
that he is deaf and dumb, and could remain so,
to the many songs not yet his to sing.

ELEGY FOR GREGORY

Gregory, I watch the moments pass.
The late October rain is music now,
And pain and hope are laid out on the grass.

Not seen or heard, that sun to which you bow,
Walking ahead into a mystery.
But here, October rain is music now,

And what is seen and heard remains for us
Both sweetness and confusion. Help us remember,
Gregory, to watch our moments pass.

And questions come that leave us less and less
Willing to say the All is what is seen,
For pain and hope both flourish in the grass.

The blackened river moving down below
Your city lights at night brings vision too:
October rain is sweet, falling for you.

Oh Gregory, as we watch our moments pass,
May what we love be also what we know.
How thick the grass that grows both hope and pain,
And you are music in October rain.

AFTER THE FIELD TRIP

Shirley, the gentle tutor, found a trapped mouse
after the field trip, in the room with the backpacks.
It was caught on adhesive cardboard, streaks of blood
were on the cardboard, but the mouse was still moving,
pulling, pulling. There was strange stillness
in that white cardboard, that non-release,
and the mouse had bright black eyes.
Could we pry it off without injuring it more? No.

So Shirley carried it outside, followed
by five of our wildest boys. I stayed indoors,
passing out treats, gathering up nametags.
Looked at my watch, impatient for day's end.

Then came to, suddenly. Ran out to the playground to be
with the mouse and Shirley. To be and do I knew not what.
Where was she? Kids everywhere, running, running.
Then I found the five boys, motionless for once, in the far
corner of the playground, hanging off the fence.
Shirley's dark head was beyond them.

Shirley's hands went up, down. A pause.
Then she walked back into the yard.
She told me, "I had to do it, I couldn't let it suffer."
I told her I could not have done it. She said,
"I couldn't touch it myself, I dropped a soda can
with ice on top of it. I feel so guilty."
I told her she did right, and knew
I wouldn't have the strength to do it.

Back in the cafeteria, one of the boys pointed
to Shirley and said, "Those are the hands of a killer!"
Shirley chased him around the cafeteria.

MIDWIFERY

—at the passing of Sadie, our old family cat

Two hours before and two after
hold the body of the dying, the dead.
She is held like an infant in the blue chair,
homeward, this most perfect passing.

Oh template of breathing and the balm
of silence in living room light
from twilight into night and beyond,
with the silence so full of what is living
as what is met in death streams onward,
here by the couch and there, outside,
under sorrel and sand. And beyond. . .

Oh call the balm in the living room
afterwards, late in the night,
her love unconditional.
And all that is coming and going,
the inarticulate streaming—*perfect.*

And which of us dies, is dying,
delivered? And who is newborn?

MEMORIAL SERVICE

—for Smokey

Are the obstacles to her whole at last
vapor and roses and singing
around the vanished spark of her?
Does she listen here, she who was girl
by the campfire, wavy-haired teenager,
older woman ill and in pain,
poet, teacher, seeker?

Does she meld the reverberations
of her parts into her whole, and do so
for us still enfleshed, our hope wavering,
forced into living one frame at a time?
Has she found in her own passage what we seek?
(It is more than redemption,
it is renewed design—the meshing of liquid light
into the soul's own cloth.)

She is now more than we knew.
She is a part of the silence composed
of the sounding beyond our ears.
She is fully her own, and her poems and roses
arise like children to embrace her.
She is the seeking that we are,
and our unbound arms are open to receive.
She is saying, "For my sake and yours, never
let fall the wildfire of this moment,
and this, and this, and this..."

TRAVELING TO SACRAMENTO NEAR THE END OF 2012

(after the Sandy Hook massacre)

Lost, I drove last night beyond the twilight,
after the rainbow followed along I-80,
after the rain-green hills and fields had filled me,
drove into the rainy traffic and dark blue
of the wrong freeway. But at last drove finally
to the right road, so long it could carry me
beyond ceaseless strip malls, over the invisible
river, miles and miles into another dark,
to a street remembered, homes alight with Christmas.
Finally I was here, and the known home opened
familiar wings, enclosed me. And everything
that was before, the pain of a deeply troubled season,
began to loosen, though not quite abate.

And in the profound sleep that came that night,
something must have prayed. Because I saw in the morning
how whatever it is that helps
can take chaos, despair, sudden death
into wilder, wider air.
As onto some plain over which, in darkness,
galaxies stand still. Gathering chords of suffering,
sacred, with the rung bell
of unspeakable silence.
Then returning us
to the crucible's narrow chamber, with its dim,
imperfect, fragile, fruitful light.

IN THE NIGHT AFTER A NEAR ONE'S PASSING

Dream of a venerable old man, well-known
to the public. Others had gone, we were alone
and he was dying. He wore a green sweater and sat
at a small table, not speaking, wholly within self.
Weakening and weakening, he vomited,
I cleaned it up. His long back went slowly forward.
Then his head and arms came down on the table,
as though a schoolchild rested.
He breathed slow breaths.
Breathed the last breath
the very moment I awoke.

And I lay in something huge, dark, deep—
nothing more so. It was
saturated with itself. It was
silence like a choir.
It had no beginning or end.
Was almost thick, pregnant.
Yet spacious. Almost
a pulse.

AT CHRISTOPHER'S PASSING

—for Laura

Now and here—air on my cheeks,
too-brief cool air. The mallards retreat,
and round low leaves perhaps
speak to the lake below.
This moment's soft blur of heat
seems all there is.

Now he who could see beyond form moves
beyond to this good death,
seeming grasped from afar in the arms
of night, draped darkness over memory.

But who can doubt from the evidence of the sky
the silver rain of washing,
of perfect release?
He would welcome this.

Years ago he quoted me Rumi,
who said death is the wedding night.
And I think Christopher would now say
each moment is preparation
to let waves of sky sweep us
to a depth we could not otherwise know.

And I ask him now:
Is this seeming oblivion
the guardian of a cosmos of light?
Of spiral and return?
Of a vast, ineffable,
and perhaps most fertile sleep?

He answers not in words but in mystery.

But *you*, little words, go to where my friend is now.
Gratitude, make him grow.
Strength and his purpose, remain.
And waves of Being, undulant, hold him aloft.

❧

BLANK SHEET OF PAPER

All that the blank sheet of paper
ever asked is this:
How long will you circle
within the fond cage
of yourself,
before finding
(and wanting to find)
that the door
is always open?

FALL OF THE ELECTION, 2016

October, and my maple has partly shed herself.
Baby Emily has sprouted two teeth, her sister Leila
has lost the same two, started kindergarten.
Two weeks ago my niece made a splendid bride.
Far away and on screen, a madman takes the stage.
The scarred warrior woman opposes him.
Close to home, a pretty young mother runs for office—
at her back, the dark money avid
for our quiet neighborhood. Autumn rain
came Friday and falls, precious, all weekend.
Our coffee can pine is suddenly taller than the maple.

Emily could be walking and the maple will be bare
by Christmas, beyond the election. Emily could be walking
through all those leaves now lingering
in the backyard sky, leaves that Leila will rake,
or jump into, or hold up, or look through. Hundreds
of tired golden windows to a wintering sun.

MEMENTO MORI

—March 2020

So many times on earth we have asked,
"Is this the end?"
So many times lost too much.
So many times bound ourselves to a living
mast, buffeted by what
it seemed we could not bear.

The task is beyond us, yet unfolds
now, in the swipe of a cloth, a step onto grass,
a touch, a look, one word followed by another.
Cell unto cell we breathe
until the met fate is fulfilled.

It is to work even as our small fingers
withdraw their futile grasp on the known,
tentatively touching invisible
threads beyond the human—
threads perhaps ordered
in a perfect, inexorable dance.

It is to work until the unwilling spirit
wills itself finally to be untied
from what it holds like a child
with toys—continuity, comfort, hope
in some orderly story. Releasing all
but the mystery of *itself.* Alert in its locus,
watching. Mystery encased in mystery.
Given birth amidst chaos again and again
from fiery dark and tears of light.

THE TWILIGHT OF THE GODS

In the end it was simple: we became too busy.
Small things drew us in.
We made lists of what needed to be done.
We formed committees. We had to.
Too many swelling hordes moved below.
What was great once became routine.
Thor's hammer sounding daily across the earth.
Odin challenged in his hall by Darwin and Jesus.
And Loki, evil one, become Bureaucracy,
both mired and attired in laws.

Now, in our twilight, we look out on the light late rain.
Here and there, torn paper blows along the streets.
We are never without the sound of cars and buses.
We are never alone, as we were with the turbulent planets,
nor do we hear our voices as they echoed once
along the corridors of the stars.

We share too many things,
too many of us stranded together in the hold of the heavens.
Will we slip between its fingers and die?
Are we ourselves uncared for and unheard?
As all around, we hear the moan and ache of the myriad
souls who gather, like us, in their last evanescent twilight.
Before the memory of memory is erased.

Humbled, we ask ourselves why every creature
is meant to know exile and flight.
We are no different from the smallest.
We are now names in a story for children.
What we were, that magnitude, is unremembered.

Yet bearing this, we grow strangely great.
Our stories hidden, they go on, as we do.
And we grow, grow as we could not have believed
we could, while the sand grains darken
and gleam in the rain below without us.

※

THE WATCHER AT THE END OF TIME

I saw Time's apples spinning on their tree.
Ominous and unplucked, they had turned rogue,
no fruit for animal or human being,
no nourishment but something dense and vague
that secretly sped up and lost its flavor.
They turned uneaten to a final end,
carrying chaos under their blurred peeling.
Spinning, they stole the savor and the feeling
from anyone who, as before, might yearn
to pause and rest awhile, to pluck and eat.
And all those travelers praying to complete
their homebound journeys: I saw them fall,
spent. Unfinished. Unable to return.
Spun into nothing from the glut of all.

IN THE YEAR OF TURNING SIXTY

1) *May, with a friend gravely ill*

It is as though the river Styx comes closer
into view, and the silence of its pure
motionlessness is upon us.
It means there is nothing more to say.
And today the tears of that fall
onto the reading glasses taken up with age.
And the lips of singing, sorrow and praise
are motionless too. They could cry out
for the wholly new, or for the lost, the ill.
But they are rendered silent by the river.
And silenced too by the very
fullness of the life behind them now.
There is nothing more to say, and this
is the beginning of departure.

And the same silence comes
when there is no place else to go.
As when an old house settles on sand, its poor
foundation, and its front steps crack,
and ridges rise in the living room floor,
and the rooms seem darker now
with what once was new.
But there is no place else to go, and this too
is the beginning of departure. It is
not knowing why one came, or what, if anything,
one leaves behind. It is not knowing what is already
lost, or who, if anyone, will come next.
It is not knowing.

And our hands, in their home, take
old roses and rosemary from dark-watered vases
and crush them into the dust of that.
Carry it, scented, into this day.

2) *June*

What hangs by a thread or a heartbeat, easily lost
or broken, is the most treasured.
It is the lightly held note, it is a tremolo
issuing into open space
while a coarse wind circles the earth.

And a coarse wind circles the earth.
Threatens the very note needed.

Let them fall, briefly, the battlements
of "Claudia," "Bill," or whoever reads
these words, hoping for what words can never give.
Let it sear through us, the ice
of the world's despair, the heat of its joy.
Let both, in a flash, fill us.
Let both, for a moment, penetrate in full.
Until we can bear no more. Until we fall again
into the smallness of "Claudia," "Bill."

Oh Word, longing, call of the great continuance,
you are the heart yearning for help in its small dark room.
You are the heart not knowing how much it needs this help,
You are the heart that looks into the mirror of itself
and sees nothing known or expected.
You are the heart, that looking in the mirror of itself,
stands still. Holds and becomes a whole world,
dangerous and sublime.

3) *July*

The death of two friends on my 60th birthday

Today the firm walls of this world move
before my eyes. If I am lucky, they will go on
falling. Inner pandemonium, then silence.
The hand of the unknown takes back
its own into itself, where there is room for everything.

Who remains behind for a time rejoices
even in sorrow—the heart's panorama briefly
flooded, opened, as rains soften a garden
parched for many years.
And prayer is in the breath,
intimate, that close, repeated,
until it is known, or perhaps made true
that who has left today
and who begins again to be born
partake of one world.

4) *August*

Early morning—and there will be no memory of this.
Or will there be?
The moments of beauty are breath and heat,
as the moments of pain are no less so.
But what is left beyond echo or aftertaste?
Beyond avenues travelled thousands of times, forgetting
the end, new breath, shedding, a shimmering?
What can plumb the superficial
deeper than the one life? Deep enough to release
the most living particle of self
to its needed freedom; or the one dying,
or the sister, child, friend to her own

pure and purifying dark,
to pure and purifying light.

So we remain. Difficult to stand and stay
at the volatile shore of unknowing
while we are left to finish a story, carry it forward.
Are they imagined, these narrow confines,
repeated and familiar, that return
after a death, when time passes? Perhaps sometimes,
though seeming narrow, they bring what is new to birth.
But the emptying out at the volatile shore
is always real. Is chosen, not given.
Can only be agreed to moment by moment.

And the moment moves, it moves.
Is study, seed, assent, unraveling.
Is silence and battle cry.

We live, we go on moving.
We are stained by death
and not washed except by death.
And we set down roots in two worlds.

   5) *September*

In the true harvest of summer's final days,
we polish our old home, we gut its filled corners.
We wash woodwork, curtains, mirrors, floors,
rehang our pictures. Outdoors, we sweep the light well,
rake plum and maple leaves that dropped early
on the dry grass of long drought.
Our summer, usually cold, is humid and warm.
We leave the windows open.

Perhaps it is time.

Perhaps there is something which has lain a long time
forgotten and self-forgetting in a dank
cabinet, now newly emptied. Perhaps it rises,
stretches as never before. Pushes open
the white door that never quite closes.
Raises itself to the open window over
the kitchen sink. Gathers itself, flies out and up.
Knows it need not return.

A Lenten Journal

IT IS NOT THE NOISE OF THE CITY

It is not the noise of the city or the raven's cries
that masks the beating of our hearts.
We are like the bluebird in the grass:
he does not know his breaths are numbered.
And yet the pool from which we draw,
into which we fall, is limitless.

The redwoods never trouble
the immensity with petty sighs.
They know the summer creek bed, dry,
does not forget the creek.
Are we less than this?
Are we not breathed in and out by that
which taught the redwoods silence?

THE CREATOR'S SORROW

I held florescence of the beating world
in my many hands. Beauty and suffering
made spirals there. The dark matter swirled
slowly, chaotic, ring within ring.
The beauty too. Beholding, I was rendered
dumb—even I. And powerless to show
the liminal world between, or why all tender
breathing souls were not allowed to know,
fully, who they were. And seeing them flailing,
even I flailed. . . But again it begins,
another day in which my unfailing
call, half-heard, sounds, briefly wins
them in their spinning lives, unfathomed mirrors.
As light and hunger languish at their cores.

❧

They ask for help but still hold back,
beset with fear.
I cannot help until
they find me now and here.

Their rooms so jammed, their space so filled
with fear and doubt,
they spin in circles,
leave me out.

Yes, the dangers, rampant, loom,
but what help can I offer them
except here and now, through
silence—or the heard, touched, seen, sent
particles of my embodiment.

So may they step aside and let me
feed them, each split-open seed
watered most and only
from its utmost need.

᷾

And what else do they serve
if not the skies
reflected
in each other's eyes?

INNER CLAMOR

Ah, the Mistress of Ceremonies in her bright dresses,
all worn at once! Easy to forget she's made of cellophane,
ripped in a flash but hard to destroy.
And the desperation she keeps in the wings, ignoring
her own certain annihilation. And how she flickers,
speaks so rapidly, so movingly on so many
subjects, it is easy to not notice
she never once completes a sentence.

INNER SOBRIETY

Its radiance demands your life,
full payment against the seas
of doubt, dross, and finally death.
Abandon these
amidst all these
to suffer your own
depth and breadth.
And soundless (as in a forest)
verticalities.

ASH WEDNESDAY IN THE CITY

—for Janet Jones

From intersecting streets and birds in thin
air of freedom, with default of falling,
arise new altitudes, the masts of vision—
first beads of buds, shoots, the shock of green,
first plum and pine, unfolding rhododendron—
all, in the sun's slow shift, the words of rain,
pure shadows of a solitude, a calling
in which the spring is bargained for and won.

Oh great one in the desert, fasting, lone,
son in whom his Father was well-pleased,
entered that desert on the heels of praise,
but only after forty nights and days
of hunger, thirst, rose worthy of temptation.
Found on the precipice, in heights of thin
air, suffering to let suffering be;
vision to let it pass that stones be bread,
that good should rule this world, reverse the dead.
Instead, that we the living, streaming, should
hold close such heat, flashpoint of doubt and faith,
white heat to iron, ore redeemed to sing
pure search upon the byways of our birth.

Oh here, here, another time to trail
that good shall grieve, fall, fail, but rise
through masses, darkened, to the one unique,
through pine and rhododendron, city street,
through pure sap of silence that descends
on traffic stopped, looking, one to all,
beyond cold fields of danger onto where,
in sudden tongues of origin, we meet.

DANGEROUS GIFT

This life with its siren longing,
echo at the edge, still vibrating,
of a sharp sword newly sheathed.
Who can keep his ear close to that keening
blade who has not, at the same time, seen
the folded paper left on the floor
for him to find, the open envelope
holding his final name?

THE GARDENER IN EARLY SPRING

Drawn drunk into spring, the gardener at first
bows even to his weeds—wild onion, dandelion, sorrel.
Is awake the morning his maple begins again.
Looks to yellow mustard flowering
in empty fields by the sea.
Awaits in the rainy skies the echo
of a distant bell that reopens him
to the taproot of a living inquiry.

He has traveled many years to be here,
and the vernal summons in his body
is one of his many names.
He forgives his past, welcomes the taste unknown
in nascent fruit, revisits chambers of shadow
in the returning green.

He has labored and will go on laboring
for the gift of his own molting.
And he asks the many swallows at his feeder,
brothers in flight, to carry him now
like a seed to all the living.

MORNING PRAYER

To work and sow another day
into the body's earth, play
densities of toil and yearning,
joy, stasis, mourning
in harmonic fugue: we lock
the front door, yet again walk
down the steps and out into
the whole, waiting, a world sent to
be our very seed. On Geary Street,
the bus arrives, strangers meet,
move, see different signposts,
trail disappearing pasts
under overcast skies. Day is to trace
the echoes of cities concealed
in a magnitude of grace, revealed
slowly or suddenly as we stretch
to touch motes alive
in the breach between notes.

THE PLUM BLOSSOMS OF MID-MARCH

—following the 2011 earthquake in Japan

After calamity, silence.
And snowfall.

Grief like a tsunami
comes quickly,
withdraws slowly.
One song from myriad throats,
disharmonized.

And these
plum blossoms
outside my window,
an ocean away. . .

IMPARTIALITY
(*The Field of Kurukshetra*)

> *"For such a one, a lump of clay, a stone or a piece of gold are alike.*
> *One who is impartial to lover, friend, and foe, who is neutral among*
> *enemies and kinsmen, and equal-minded to the saint and the sinner,*
> *excels."* —Bhagavad Gita (6.8-9)

Beyond what the greatest have done and the gratitude
we pay them, the honor nourishing them even after death;
beyond what the violent ignorant have done, are doing,
cruel out of comfort, belief, avarice, or desperate youth;
beyond all that we fear (and we fear almost everything);
beyond all that has been lost (though the heart bleed),
all that is being lost even
as these words commit to ink;
beyond all that we share as the violent ignorant,
willing thieves, cruel in comfort, avarice, belief;
beyond all that in us is greatness, also shared;
beyond, beyond all this:

Each morning, heartbreak and quiet exultation
meet again to vie on the grassy field
where timeless battles have already been pitched—
each warrior, past or present, a blade of grass.

Oh moment in the dark of day, unlocked recess
shedding your contents, sacred wound
spilling your players into the vortex of the play:

Be the still hand held on the hard-beating heart
of the Witness, who came as grass to see—
that one who is bladed, small, trampled
by heavy feet, blown in every direction.
But who is rooted. Inside whom is all
that has already been done and undone.

Until he joins the wind that bows him,
until he joins the wind that blows him,
until he grows to see from everywhere—

hold your hand on his pounding heart.
Keep it there.

ATTAR OF TIME

"Thus the superior man does not permit his thoughts
to go beyond his situation." —the I Ching

Attar of time
mind quiet
heart still
hot will cool
on altar of thyme
woodruff
sage I will be

oh alter the time
in my gold bottle
seal
hot will
into heart
mind
in still

altar of gold
will of warm attar

in cool
given
stillwater

THE GREATER AND LESSER SEEING

In a dream, angry, I drifted into one corner
of a small room. And there for a moment stood
tasting what I was. Trailing the raw look
was a lion tamer's chair in my hands,
as if anything at all could keep back
the living harsh force of what I saw.

In the vast mind, what is wounded
that cannot find its way in dignity
to the promontory of its own vastness,
looking out, down, everywhere,
and at each thing? I remembered that sometimes
anger prepares the self for its next
and perhaps most needed action.
Though raw light on that self, like an uncovered
light bulb, is not yet the sun's largesse.

&

RAIN IN LATE LENT

Nothing left of winter now. But to keep covenant
awhile longer with some vast pulse of pain,
fatigue, need, is inexplicably to invite
fruit from the stagnant branch, whole from fragment,
and one's own culled, called song to unite
with this long wild bloom of rain.

PALM SUNDAY

In the same way it seems that breath and earth
could last forever, the starry worlds hide from us
in plain sight—concealed from day
by cold sunlight after rain,
from night by the lights of the city.

Meanwhile, the disappearing foam reforms,
the silver snail-trail is washed
to new completion by late rain,
the ramparts of the sea consent to break
again and again in cold rhythms of eternity.

What in us can bear the awakening
that descends on us briefly, another world
we enter but briefly?
What in us can bear this mandala,
so austere with beauty,
the unspeakable mathematics of truth,
and so radiant with what
has everything and nothing to do with us?

A LENTEN JOURNAL

Bloom scent everywhere.
Why, with earth drunk on herself,
must we keep sober?

These schoolgirl calla
lilies. Curved, clean, swaying, not
ever touching mud.

Cypress fell in last
December's storm. Roots clutching
air, huge. I look away.

Do we look for home,
or listen? Silence taking
the form of new leaves.

—the week in February both a friend and our
daughter's kitten died

One week, two loved ones
gone. Yet still believing
I belong to myself.

Her little cat died
suddenly. Pure love gone back
to the atmosphere.

Human sacrifice?
Welcoming the ache of pure
love amid sorrow.

Conscience in the wake
of loss. Even stray weeds want
to begin again.

Nothing to fear in
this quiet house but the ache
of not having *seen*.

And the morning gulls,
the grass, the damp weeds, all say,
"Who dares to see, loves."

I lay sleepless till
it alighted: care of self
and the endless source.

Time-change in Lent:
how tree, pen, street, dish each said,
"*All your time is here.*"

St. Dominic's on
Good Friday. Strangers, hundreds,
akin in silence.

                              And what is courage
                              now? Only to pause. Myself
                              and the wild onions. . .

Suite for Persephone

The dark begets the light and the light begets the dark in
ceaseless alternation. . .

—Treatise on the I Ching

. . .among cantadoras it is called the wise or knowing nature. It
is sometimes called the "woman who lives at the end of time" or
the "woman who lives at the edge of the world"
. . .always a creature-hag, or a death Goddess,
or a maiden in descent. . .

—Clarissa Pinkola Estes

SUITE FOR PERSEPHONE

1) Her Words to Demeter from the Land of the Dead

Mother, do not allow the appetite of your love
into the arbor of my dreams, where I released you long ago.
You've studied the path of spiraling roses, you know
that what lives amidst everything, unfolds alone.
But though I've released you, I have never left you.
I am gathering for you the greening blossoms,
and I am giving you the dying blossoms.
Feed them all to the diaphanous bird
who carries these words up to you, and beyond,
to a distance of cold comets. That far they rise
above the crags and skies of the dead,
filled with my voice.

Yes, at times in my anger,
I throw behind the pillows of another night,
ignore the known sounds under the door,
let fly blows of both spirit and heart.
I am not reflected in the glass surrounding me,
nor am I wasted among the acacias above.
Everything falls away from me now.
I don't know if my steps have found
the next hollow in the mountain of my life,
or truly, whether I rise or fall.

And yet, over time, unexpectedly,
my bruised feet grow nourished by these sands.
Do not fear for the metallic blossoms Death
has torn into my hands—hands which also receive
the light feathers of the future.
For I am the seed, always,

and I understand the promptings of my path.
To be so empty, cuplike in the night,
that I am swept and cleansed by this black wind
beneath your seas. Not forgetting your lissome weeds.
Not slighting your vines, your trees, because I die
to become them all. Watching whole worlds
lose and retrieve themselves.
Turning your grief into grass.

2) *Her Words to Hades*

Half-dreaming, half-sleeping beside you, I have lain
amidst huge thoughts and small ones, hoping to hear
the very greatest, but hearing everything instead.

Everything at once is not easy.
Sometimes I plunge and drift, repeating
words half-known, or words said too often.
Sometimes I glimpse the patterns
of a vast life I have lost to solidity.
But you, my blossoming and defeat,
are one thing constant.

Oh you, you: how have I found you again?
As I listened for you once in my nightmare,
now I watch for you in the bold depth
of every mirror—anything to know you well,
as I await what must transfigure me.
What was *I*, I wonder, before you claimed me?
Before I became for you, in the play of forces,
caught and grown, like water brimming up
to finally flood your parched, expendable home?
We each hold only a shard of what we were.

But now, between embraces, let us honor
that secret word we share, that word we've formed.
It has stayed too long in the cold eddies
of the brain, afraid to enter the heart's fray.
It is the one sound that will be heard
by both the living and dead.
One day it may unite them all.
For this I've placed paired wings
above our bed, properly weighted
to tame the agitated birds within us both.

Sometimes I am a wanderer who has ventured
to the far borders of a dream, and then been found
alive again. Sometimes I fall and fall,
weightless, into hollow circles of myself.
But always I hear your whisper, urgent: "*Love,
do not fear the long, repeated lakes of chaos.*"

3) *Despair*

It is a loud darkness I go into.
I too am among the stark, deluded bodies.
I see everything I've feared to be, and so become
the rage of a world turned in on itself,
killing what it makes. I become the miasma.

And I become them all, become the grey-faced men
cast out of themselves in youth.
Become the children who leave no one
to mourn them on the mountain,
the old women on whose bitter spirits
the living still drip their acid anger.

And I become the pock-marked faces
who made petty all that hope and faith
meant to tell them. They bottled it, warm,
like the blood drained from small animals.
They sold it to others for profit.

I become those too who ache for what was never
theirs, those pulled by rooms, the implosion
of rooms crowded with objects, memories,
all of which stayed over time.
These unslaked ones cannot empty themselves
enough to breathe. Their doors have locked.
"Give us air!" I cry with them.

And I become others who remember
what was waiting for them in the heather,
with the soldiers walking toward them in their boots.
They cannot forget the sound of their own screams.
They dwell in their death,
they are immured in the memory of death.
They cannot find their lost volition.

Finally, I come to the harrowing cliff
where the soul's buzzards circle, awaiting the end.
How quietly they sit, those with no hope,
looking down, heads bent as though in prayer.
Soft music plays in the air. They do not hear.
Their excrement dries on the cement.

And I weep for the starved creatures of this night,
cold on their boughs, who would happily lap
the water from each other's eyes.
They do not know I have entered them.
Like them, I am loosened on the air before my time,

unprepared to die, hover, and be taken
to the small blue world of the summoned.

And time is short, and the kingdom of our being
is overrun by invaders from all sides.
And the sloth of the heart is telling us
we will never absorb the herb of becoming,
though the plants grow everywhere around us.
And there is no perfection anywhere
that like a crawling thing, minute, has not
been brushed apart by our fingers.

And the small, imprisoned self holds forth,
as always, to its four walls. It is waiting
for a trial which may never come.
It can never, even if it wished,
be left for dead.

I ask:
for what is pain the payment?

4) *She Joins with the Dead in Meditation*

Now there is nothing left but listening.

And so I listen, amidst myriads of shadows,
sharing the chambers of a solitude
each could believe his own.

At first we are confused by too many words,
words in the brain like piles of leaves
blown everywhere, briefly raked,
blown everywhere again.

We know real words are not like this
retraction into the shallow-watered dunes,

this flotsam of the returning, turning mind
in the cold, pinched motions of its night.

But everything dreaded once has come to pass
here, now, and in the mind's vacancy
before the half-memories of what we were.
For long ago, we lost the flora of ourselves.
We had forgotten to weed it, having removed
only the smallest florets of delusion.

Now we listen.

We listen at the root of ourselves.

We listen, hoping to enter
a sacrifice which is never twice the same.
For which the rigid turn to soft clay.
From which the blooming worlds emerge.

And listening, we protect ourselves from nothing.
We absorb and endure the sharpness
of the sweetness of a honey
beyond reach of human longing.

We know that in the world above, the vineyards
have begun to fall, inviting the fingers of the wise
to remember their own dark fruit.
But here, with wounded eyes, we go on seeing.
Knowing our sacrifice is incomplete,
and the vision sought may not reveal itself,
nor our raging fires ever cease.

But here, now, and in the memory of what
we are, we touch our new, emergent faces
in the backward-turning mirror of our silence.

5) *Vision*

I was born to live between many worlds.
In the outcropping over the sea
and in your dark hallway.
In the grey fields of late afternoon
and under the skies before a storm.
The ribbon of larvae under the bushes
and the planets' dance both meet in my blood.
All so that my gnarled, dank body
may, under your feet, grow fragrant,
and my transformation
open the plums to your lips.

Yes, I too have hurried to meet what is next,
ignoring the waiting garden in which
a larger voice could infuse me.
Like you, I have balked before greatness.
But I know now there is no chance awakening.
Only the endless payment, with or without us,
for a universe of birth, wedding, unraveling.

And you who burn your thresholds as well as bridges,
who take too much into an otherwise empty night:
you cannot bear what I put into your hands,
the seemingly indigestible
night-nourishment precious as sunlight.
But what is there to fear and where to run?
We are both the weak who enter the garden
on our knees, and the strong who do not die.
Yet always pursued by the narcissus
of our very first longing.
We plucked it once and will do so again.
It opened us to death but did not itself die.

It opens us still to the arc arising
equally over dawn and annihilation.

I only take from you what is not needed.
It will be humus, aster, ash,
the selves you used, then shed.
I only take what you have borrowed.
But you have borrowed almost everything.

Yet whatever else the cold night issues,
the storm moving in from the east is harbinger
of inexplicable hope.
I invite this, always.

And I stand guard at your doorway.
keep your deepest home untrammeled,
for it awaits only you. Brush back
the heavy cloth that protects you,
the words, forms, fears
shielding you from what you know,
and from what is unknown.
Tomorrow rain will open the garden, but now,
my schism in the earth is yours to enter.

In me, nothing is wasted.
In me, there is everywhere to alight.

I am the shadow at the heart of your changing.

The Holiday Annals of Frankie Catchild

Who Was *Frankie?*

If Nikos Kazantakis had written a cat into his novels, it would have been Frankie. Our spectacular calico, a feline knock-out, was by nature and nurture Greek. Frankie and her *very* different bosom companion Pickle—a trim, shy, cerebral tabby—were raised early in life by Greek-American women. Frankie was like these beautiful women, only more so. She was big, aggressively affectionate, the center of any gathering. She was especially fond of men, but if necessary would lick anyone in sight. If this happened to be Pickle, that prim tabby was acutely embarrassed.

Holidays were a problem. Frankie was a avowed pantheist, and any religious holiday made her even more excitable. Christmas was the worst. Wrapping presents with Frankie in the room was almost impossible. Shiny ribbon, rippable wrapping paper, and humans attending to something other than her drove her wild.

So near Christmas 2012, just before the world was scheduled to end, we locked Frankie in our office sunroom with a pile of food, a houseplant to munch on, a fly or two to chase—supplies enough to last until the presents were wrapped. The next day, to our surprise, sheets of computer paper were slipped out from under the door, with the first of Frankie's holiday poems, "Holiday Cat Doggerel!" Amazingly, Frankie had an accurate grasp not only of family but of current events. Along with cozy holiday images, she offered alternate plans in case the world didn't end—all at the level of verse truly warranting the term "doggerel." We were amazed!

Inspired by her success and already skilled at treading on keyboards, she soon started her own Facebook page. The surname "Catchild" completed her *nom de plume*. Two Christmases later, she opened her psychic channels in a poetric ode to Pickle, exploring her life partner's remarkable past lives throughout history.

But sadly, Frankie passed away in July 2017. We deeply mourned our over-the-top friend, even as Pickle seamlessly assumed the role of Most Adored. Then a Christmas miracle occurred near the end of 2018. A rolled vellum scroll appeared on our floor under an open window, printed in glowing gold letters. Another holiday epistle from Frankie! It appeared she'd been closely watching us from the Other Realm. Wow, how lucky were we??! Frankie was still around, and in her homage to family far from silent—even in this, her abridged version. How we appreciated a glimpse of the truly Big Picture from our large, big-hearted, departed friend.

So here are Frankie's Holiday Annals, in all their glory. Enjoy!

HOLIDAY CAT DOGGEREL!

Greetings, loved ones, sea to peak,
From a Celtic kitty and one who's Greek!
The luscious Frankie, and Pickle too,
Send catfelt cheer to all of you!
What's holidays without a toddy
That's custom-made for any body??
Consider that when you read this ditty.
Your bartender might be a kitty!

Yes, we made our list for Santa:
Mice to chase (but not with hanta!),
Ribbon, tuna, catnip, sun,
Legnaps, playfights for some fun.
But if you think we just lie curled
In a cat-o-centric world,
Think again! We *look* immobile
But our powers could go *global*!
Pickle's wild Druidic spell
Follows Frankie's Delphic tail!
Can't change all from runes and rappin'
But who knows what could *really* happen??!

Mayan calendar ends – okay!!
Tomorrow is another day!
Hamas, Israel might not tiff.
Feather bed under fiscal cliff??
Long, long life to Dalai Lama,
Hand in hand, Repubs., Obama.

Roof overhead! Food on the table!
Paying work as long as you're able!
Living like kitties (fair weather or sad),
Minute by minute— *it's not that bad!*

And simple joys for everyone.
Insight! Humor! Music! Fun!
And don't forget long baths, warm hats,
Good health, great hugs, and petting cats!
For all your friends, grannies, fathers,
Precious babies, mates, mothers,
Cousins, aunties, cat and dog,
Brothers, sisters—*another log!!!*
We might not know what all this means
But help is just behind the scenes!
And when low spirits come to you,
We say, "Don't droop! Be like unto
Us window kitties, young and old.
WE'RE HERE TO WATCH IT ALL UNFOLD!!!"

    —December 2012

PICKLE'S CHRISTMAS ROOTS!!

Hey, little tribe, a fond "Hurrah!"
As Frankie takes her pen in paw
To write of Pickle, short-haired, clean,
Her true Life Partner, her Kitty Queen!!!
The Ages of Pickle are many and great,
More lives than nine to test her fate!
Let's put out Greek oracular shoots
To check out Pickle's Christmas roots!
One hop on Father Time's own lap,
One plunge into a Cosmic Nap,
And ahhhh, Pickle, I start to see
Your long Decembers' history!!
From Ice Age Kitty to Metro Cat,
A little of this, a little of that. . . !

. . .You're tickling a flea on Adam's fig,
Tangling a French King Louis' wig!!
Snug between Henry and his wives
(But keeping your head through all your lives!!).
Scratching Cromwell. . ."by accident!"
In Nero's sandwich making a dent!!
Getting a pat from Genghis Khan,
Not getting eaten in Dynasty Han!!
With Moses, sharing bagels and lox,
With Plato, thinking "outside the box!"
Switching your tail to troubadour lilt!
Peeking under Prince Charlie's kilt!!

And wowing Cleopatra, too,
(Until you snag a veil or two!!!)
But most you shine in Celtic times,
Through moor, mist and mountain climes!!
Keeping a priestess cozy and warm,
Mangling a mouse in calm and storm!
Purring at Stonehenge, "pushing" at Bath,
"Helping" a Druid with his math!!
Oh Church of England cat, who knew
What pagan fires burn in you??!!

But here, my Pickle, in Christmas Now,
I only want to sing out "Wow!!!"
The glory of your cat-lives brings
Contentment rich in simple things!
So let's shred ribbon, disrupt some wrapping!
There's more to life than Cosmic Napping!!!

Oh Jane Austen to my Marilyn Monroe,
Come sit within the fire's glow
With Teddy, Gaga, Leila, more,
With kith and kin that we adore,
With creatures near, in distant places,
Fin, feather, flesh or furry faces!!
Inscrutable tabby, Pickle I've picked,
Let's be the Licker and the Licked!!
And to New Year and Old keep sending
HAPPY BEGINNING, HAPPY ENDING!!!

    —December 2014

FRANKIE LOOKS DOWN ON HER PEEPS FROM A PORTHOLE IN HEAVEN!!!

The Moon is far, the Stars are full,
And I'm past feather, fur, and wool!
But that can't stop this ghostly kitty
Materializing another ditty!
Heaven's a place I can't describe,
But let's just say, my little tribe,
It's *w-a-y-y-y* beyond my wildest dream
Of Frankie's own *GREEK SOCCER TEAM!!!*

Now, as your holidays draw nigh,
I'm looking down with catly eye,
And take in paw my heavenly pen
To blazon greetings once again!
Foremost and first, I toast my Pickle,
Tabby as yet untouched by Sickle!
Oh Pickle, faithful kitty mild,
You're happy to be an only child!
There's football, petting, nary an "ouch"
Blissed out with "Teddy" on the couch!!
Jane Austen kitty, you've found *your* place
Where I don't take up all the space!!!

Meanwhile, grandgirls circle round.
Emily's learned to *STAND HER GROUND*,
Firm that she'll wear only dresses!!
Leila June's grown out her tresses,
And her coterie—I'd span it
Possibly *beyond* the planet!!!!

Rams and Anne, we toast your love!
Blessed-tired-hardworking? ALL the above!!
We're glad New Orleans offered magic,
Rex Sox games did not prove tragic!!
"Mommy, Daddy," much-loved two,
Your girls and family honor you!!

Now onto loved ones far afield.
(This time/space thing has *GOT* to yield!)
And on our journey's farthest leg,
We fly to see sweet Clara and Greg!!!
Wedding recovery (whew!) complete,
In Ireland now they plant their feet.
We miss them (sniff) but so glad they
Have work they *love*—hip, hip, hooray!!

. . .But best to shorten up this raga!
We'll just pop in on Pop-Pop, Gaga.
Pop-Pop, a.k.a. Billy, Teddy,
For his RETIREMENT makes ready!
Door hardware, 4 a.m., and whew!
This boy deserves the *TRULY NEW*!!
And Gaga's life, though *slightly* busy
(Saunas, Stow Lake dispel tizzy)
Keeps her out of hanky-panky—
The better to channel darling Frankie!!!

SOOO many more not oded here
But still among those near and dear!
And yup, the times aren't easy-peasy,

The headlines won't exactly please ye,
But *DON'T* let heads that just keep talking
Put gloom and doom inside your Stocking‼
Fires 'n' floods, coyotes on Geary—
No one could say it's dull or dreary!
And Chinese curse might prove sublimes:
"Be BLESSED to live in interesting times‼!"

Well, even this non-finite kitty
Must find some way to end her ditty!
So ringside seat or high-up glory,
Whatever you do, *DON'T MISS THE STORY‼*
This Yin/Yang thing just won't stop changing‼
Wow, our cells are *rearranging‼!*
But Frankie says, "It's BIG up here!
SO BE OF STOUT HEART‼ BE OF GOOD CHEER‼!!"

—*December* 2018

Each Day is a Living God of Time

EACH DAY IS A LIVING GOD OF TIME

—from the Maya, who worshipped Time

Yes, I may die in a small room, and worse,
in some pinched space of myself
where no sky enters, where fear and pain
are all, and the first gull-sound
of the infinite is mistaken
for an old refrigerator's creak.

But to knock now on the half-locked door
opening out of the petty, the pinched,
into the heart's green soil-way,
its spring-source, flame, and river:

Is it too much to ask of this seemingly
modest day, which again arrived perfectly
over our beds and houses, with time's taper
lit, gold and great, munificent,
even while melting away?

ADAM

This garden was not given him to master
stardust and amoeba, bird and beast,
with his telescopic, microscopic sight.
But rather, with that sight to foster, slowly,
each pregnant element. He breathed its least
signature into virgin forms of light.

Explorer, mathematician, scientist
and naked one ecstatic in the trees,
knew genesis as innocence and gift,
said "roots" and roots appeared, unfolded, kissed
the inward soil as soma that released
that nascent garden. Saw first flowers lift,

color on color, spectrum strung to space
in endless facets, spirals, and beginning.
How could he sleep for knowing, before he touched
the fruit untasted in that verdant place,
exploding beauty in its newness, fanning
all time to come before his eager face?

And what began as garden, laboratory
of animal and holy molecule,
sang in his cells as world, reverberant stone,
a primal question and an arc of glory,
magnetized. And earth, unblemished jewel,
was galvanized. Was shaken to the bone.

THE ESOTERIC

What flower given to work,
what fragment in the dust, always
waiting, nourishing, the nourished,
will not be lost?

And what same hidden flower
again trembles, again dies in dust
at untold cost, a death
known to so few, wounding so many?

And again, below cacophony,
what is lost—that almost
inaccessible body rising
in tragic murmur? Barely
amidst the masses a breath,
shade of a greatness even
their young children have forgotten.

Heart, do not turn, tragic,
to find too late
above and below the loud
force field of man's earth,
home in which secretly,
in bold hope, you burn to birth.

THE GREAT QUESTION

This path
shifts beneath my feet.
How will I recognize
one who protects me
from myself?

❧

THE GREAT UNFOLDING

(*after* Waters of the Afternoon, 2010)

Now, feasting on gratitude,
I leave its tender crumbs
in my open hands
for the One
who carries my changing
future under his wings.

SOUL AND SACRIFICE

Rainless winter,
and there she was
on Sunday morning,
the first week of spring.
Perfect monarch butterfly
almost perfectly still.
It had showered in the night
and she lay, for all to see,
on wet brown concrete
just outside the laundry room.
Dying and ashine.

DAY IN OCTOBER NEAR REDWOODS

This earth, a hard school.
But how soft the autumn soil
after last week's rain. . .

Creek bed, when will rain
cover all the dry stones of
your sleeping body?

Is this silence heard
among the redwoods their own
loud conversation?

—while looking at a redwood stump

Stillness. Turbulence.
Bleached, dark contortion. Time's slow
perfect violence.

Taller, more sedate
than human, these green spears.
But rimmed in red light.

Never seek haiku
at the cost of silence or
shamrocks in fall light.

Oh bright yellow one,
bobbing with friends, do you know
you're a tiny sun?

Oh yellow ones, bright,
don't you know you are All Suns
to our waning light?

Who can be calm when
yellow flowers cry such loud
spring in October?

Between Holy God,
Holy Firm, even this redwood
knows not who it is.

Marveling how sunlight
suddenly finds this shadow
writing in silence.

OF JACOB AND THE ANGEL

*"Isn't it the great tragedy, when wrestling with God, not to be
defeated?" —Simone Weil*

Will everything be taken away, and soon?
Who prepares for the emptying
as he hovers under stars, a moon,
the ancestral great ones waiting?

In the precious body which meets
a world of forces, holds them
in chaos or in dance, greets
or withstands their whim,

who listens for the constant battle cry
between the angel and the man?
Who accepts to try
shedding the blood of his own human?

Who is it that finally stays?
He struggles, dissolves, yes, to remain.
In the tolling of lives and days,
transformed. *And his work is not in vain.*

WHAT WORK REMAINS UNDONE

What work remains undone?
So near it can't be seen.
So close it can't be said.

Inhabiting, unmoved,
or flickering, unstill—
is it not the same
unraveling? Briefly
the ball of thread
is gathered, round and readied.
And then again dropped.

It's happening this moment,
and unto death and beyond.

What needed work, unseen,
is never done,
never done?

REMORSE (THE LISTENER)

Was a question answered too quickly.
Had good intentions.
Saw us drain into ever smaller worlds.
Is hunger, anger, act, delight in the act.
Then another biting down,
but now *we* are the bitten.
Doesn't swallow or cough us up.
Just keeps us. Rolls us at leisure
in an unhungry mouth.

> *During illness, from her kitchen, my friend*
> *watched two bluebirds make a nest.*
> *And a new male came one day, fought*
> *the father. She was sure he'd die and ran out*
> *onto her patio, clapped her hands, yelled,*
> *stopped the fight. But the parents flew off,*
> *never returned. A line of ants streamed*
> *in and out of the dead cracked eggs.*

Confounds, is simplicity itself.
Goes and comes back, a spiral.
Is always near.
Is a vise of light, of lightning.
May be uncovered. May be carried, sacred.
May carry us into thunder, new.
Has all the time in the world.
Lets us know we do not.

> *The Listener exudes the scent*
> *of manna, amidst excrement.*
> *And holds closer than flesh his force,*
> *and bathes in nectar of Remorse.*

NOT THIS BREEZE

Because I am not
this breeze shaking
the cobweb under my window,
I will never know what path
the sky takes to reach me,
or what in the wind
inhabits me like a seed.

THE SOUL'S STORY IS NEVER READ IN ONE SITTING

—after Deepa Mehta's film Water

The soul's story is never read in one sitting.
Is not spread out on the ground, is not a paragraph
in the Sunday paper with a youthful picture.
The soul's story is learned in the suffering
of a clouded mirror. The housewife and soldier
both shed tears of blood, bile to the indigestible.
It is a shedding in which tumors of the heart
are washed away. It is the third flood given us to bear.

The numinous sorrow of the soul rises up
over shattered doors and the almost certain
drop into defeat. Its arc is always unknown.
It is the long-dead stars whose light
we only now see. It is the blue irises by the lake
which die by May, but whose foliage glows
green through summer. The soul is described
by its circle of numinous sorrow.

The stories of the soul are learned one by one,
learned by heart. The bearded man near the corner
store, his styrofoam box open for coins,
and the little monk in a Himalayan cave
both come to comfort in the company
of the vast, which is surprised by nothing.
They are each the core of the beginning
of a sun, breathing its story.

After midnight the soul wakes to the sound
of its story. The overtones move near the piano,
in the wall behind the bed, the upstairs floorboards.

They blow through the pine tree by the fence,
they enter with resolution clear as a newborn's cry,
and as commanding. Framed in the dark,
they offer dissolution, great and sweet.
So that for the moment everything unneeded,
not the heart of the story, falls away.

Thus the soul begins hearing itself recorded.
Slowly learns not to run from the sound
of its own voice. Sees that earth is never drained
of the sacrifice needed for light.
Fills its place by the window and in the street.
Takes seed and hammer, lover and child in hand.
Tastes mercy as intimate fruit,
the help given by a wounded universe.

And its mantra and koan are one and the same:
"*Alone, alone,*" it cries, "*And never alone!*"

ON "A NEW CONCEPTION OF GOD"

—Boulder 2010

Something new?
Little words, don't tangle me up
in all your leashes.

"Way of no esape."
Come on in!
There's plenty of room
in the crucible!

In the image of God,
to bear witness.
Prayer and Despair. . .

How can I ponder
man's possibility
and let the lilacs only graze me?

Hey you two!
Resourceful, ever-hungry wolf,
tender sheep, you follower,
don't you know *I'm* here?

A cup of tea in the sun—
what's the risk?
Joy. Yet everything is at stake.

Fear, dried-up thoughts
flooding my moments.
Oil spill of the heart.

A particle of the sorrow
of the Creator—
am I ready for that?

And I thought it was only me:
Cloud, tree, mountain, lilac, squirrel
all feel themselves as *I*.

The Peaches of Immortality

THE HEART BEFORE THE WINTER SOLSTICE

Our new gold curtains,
glowing in August,
are now too thin for December.
It seems they cover the windows
but not the heart.
They let in all
the world's suffering,
so heavy a wind
that every organ in the body
revolts, cries out, drops back,
falls even more hidden into its recess.

All but the heart itself
which is truly unsheltered.
It stands in the living room naked,
doubting the suns of its native land.
Stranded between what it sees
and what it knows.
Perceiving day through thin fabric
but unsure of its power to meet
the parting of curtains,
so cold, cold this light.

QUESTION AND QUEST

Peer out into the wild evening. See
the play of forces in the dyed dusk.
Earth kneaded in her blue bowl.
Oblivion and the death-dark egg.
Intermittent storm, and beyond form, breathing. . .

It is an inland ocean we walk into,
down a sloped beach, a dropping-off where
it is not known how we will return.
Having discovered we already hold
wind, whale, anemone, fire, house,
anger, faith, city, skyway, mountain.
And freely releasing (if not becoming)
the homing birds who have waited
to be born for just this moment.

THE WATER OF LIFE

That which flows apart, in impassable places,
or so near it cannot be seen. Which is at first
drunk alone. Which is science and art, absolution,
an overflowing cup. Which we drank as a child
with crayon and paper, hands on the keys,
raised voices, bare feet. Which later
we are driven back to in desperation.
Which accords with our daily bread.

Which we wish to share, it is always meant to be
passed on in a great and further feast.
But which flows despite the human—the large
refusal, dismissal, disdain, doubt,
the outright violation. Which lives, lives.
Survives praise, the accolade of the mass.
Survives solitude, the mass turned murderous.
Prevails over fatigue, is insight from illness.
Is sacred grief.

Is the study we were made for, were meant
to be given. Is offering: water and wine.
Wants us to stay thirsty. Will drain into the sediment
of the earth, will evaporate over cities.
Is goblet and bath. Is ever moving.
Makes of us an ablution for the next dweller,
and the next, and the next.
Is the very smallest note heard
by those watching, listening ones.
Echoes far beyond the amphitheater.

THE BUDDHA'S PALM

If Monkey, with his great cloud somersaults,
could not vault it, why should we expect to land
anywhere but home? But we walk out early
the last evening in December, hoping against hope
any sidewalk will lead us to our true path.
We go down into the backyard, a winter garden
where blackberry vines have overcome
the grass we once planted by hand.
We tend what we can these days, but we too
are cracked asphalt, grass overcome,
and in time will be more so. We ask:
Who answers our footfall, our coming and going?
Isn't search our long circumference,
and every arrival a new night of search?
Kneeling, we are left holding in our own
minute palms only the humus, dark and sweet,
that was never of our making.

And courage, a wing-flash, descending.

PRAYER AMONG REDWOODS

—for Jim George

How long and late
these ancient roots
coil round my being.
Will what I cannot see
ever find its way
into the light?

I am so far
from that one sound
I asked for long ago,
so close
to what I cannot say.

Some master work,
willing to be embodied,
refuses against all odds
to be forgotten.

"Wait, wait," I ask
of each tree in the grove,
and the sky beyond.

Oh my roots,
in the void
luminous beyond speech,
take hold.

FOR SOPHIA'S POT

—after returning from England, 2009

Each morning I look down at what she made me,
the clay spiral below indigo space,
dark vessel within day's colors.
(It will again be one with the night.)
But today I am one returned home
after a spacious journey, again narrowed
by fears and worry, all my windows painted shut.
Sophia's pot holds nothing, there is nothing
to hold, and nothing to see but blue.
Yet mountain, stone, the sleeping soil,
man and woman, city, sky,
ocean and succulent earth, all meet
here in her impartial chamber.

(Once, briefly, a rind of fruit
fell open in my hungry hand. And the space
was gold, was my true compass,
human compass.
Then, as it had come, it was gone.
And my hand is hungry again.)

Oh landscape, indigo one, rendered into silence,
let fall in me that power
in which dark home is known
and its domain retrieved.

The taste of sorrow in the mouth
has joined with the fragrance of joy
to birth an abundant shore, a new and secret sense:
the blue equipoise of continual release.

AND STILL THE CHOIR REMAINS

And still the choir remains
that calls the hidden stems
to grow, and calls the rains
to wash the mud from gems

left for us long ago.
The masters' mysteries,
the choir and its echo,
world-speed and rusted keys

all fall to us, abundant.
Abundant: drought, rain,
dispersion, and the rampant
found voices in refrain.

MUSIC

That sorrow and joy, in ceaseless counterpoint
Descend, then weave, then weld us to a love
Hopeless but ecstatic: there we await,
In that love's sounding, awed, *ourselves*—not above
Dissonance but within it, listening.
Listening as the years intone a scale
Impelling us, in urgent hastening,
To tap the waters of a deathless well;
Listening as each mote of sound is sung,
Penetrates the apertures, the skin;
As out of life and death one bell is rung,
Attuning us beyond ourselves; then
Configuring, from our dissonance, heat and light—
The last and sweetest notes to our cold night.

OF THE MAGI

1) *Melchoir*

I am quite sure this work will never be known,
and yet I speak. It was beyond our apprehension.
At first, each of us was alone with the Child.
I saw my own face, as the others did, in his own.
He looked back at me a long time.
Memories of youth and childhood flooded me.
I stood quite still in my body.
The Mother's eyes were joy and sorrow.
I was old then, but now am a tree of such winter,
I can no longer hide myself for my bare branches.

Later, we all three entered his presence together.
Which gift would he choose?
Gold, and he would be a king;
myrrh, a healer; frankincense, a god.
Equally with his small hands he received them all.
And offered us gifts of his own—three boxes,
each holding a plain grey stone.
We bowed low to him, and took our leave.

We traveled the byroads home, and the stones
grew heavier. They seemed without any value,
even from him. Pausing, we dropped them to the ground.
Each stone burst into flames, and faith
sealed itself into our beings, unbreakable.

Some months later, I awoke from a deep sleep,
unaccountable radiance coursing every limb.
I knew then, briefly, how the sun could pulse
through a human form. Could even, for a lifetime, become it.

We three still speak of all this.
In the language of the heart, we speak together from afar.
We know the dangers in the human home
cannot be measured. Again and again, implacable winds
blow down the inmost temple.
But he is manifest. We have taken what is
into our bodies. At the slough of despair,
we give praise. We worship fire.

And I taste my life becoming a clay chalice,
cracked down the middle, like everything human, yet tipped
to give and receive, ever more freely,
the water and wine of many worlds.

I am learning to swallow light.

2) *Balthazar*

What is clear to me now, in the autumn of time,
is work. Young and old turn to me for strength.
I have not traveled far enough to rest.
I cannot set down the burdens of many years.
And every day the imprint of death, that coldly
intricate design, is more clear on the palm of my hand.

Yet the Child I have seen, who himself
may never know middle age, has seen me.
Through him I study the secret of what is *between*:
what it means to apprehend imperceptible
movement. And sometimes to suffer it.
As in shades between stasis and wonder.
Between the dancer's lifted arm and the watcher's heart.
Between what the sitar knows and what is intoned.
Between the locked gazes of opposing warriors,
dying at each other's hands.

The Child himself, after death and between dimensions,
will live almost three days, perhaps three eons,
in the viscera of worlds, in the absolute
of black, imploding space. Three days
in anything like that dark, and a man
could understand all mysteries.

I am far, far from this. And yet I practice:
hoping, hour by hour, to bear witness,
ever more disillusioned and illumined;
to meet entropy at every turn, and still
uncover chambers of silence in the body.

And I know my burdens are like bags of gold—
dead weight if not shared treasure. I would bear them
as a woman carries a heavy jar on her head:
she has learned, gladly, never to move in haste.
Later she will share the contents of her jar.

One releases much by this age, and will be asked
to release more. Does gratitude live amidst this,
its ore untapped? Does time distill us?
If so, what happens between drops?
Can a man narrowed by age taste
the free fall of the infinite and not turn back?

I have asked all this of him, and wordless he has said,
"*You must learn to see in the dark.*"

3) *Caspar*

Let the youngest speak last, for my task
is the most difficult of all: to carry forward.

There were many urgent dreams before the Child's birth.
He appeared, luminous, in different forms—

a baby boy or girl, or fragile winged being.
Too often ignored, untended, yet smiling at me.
And how easily, in my earlier surge
to be and do all, I could have trampled him.

Now I have received some particle of his magic,
have received the imperative of his magic.
Would live this change among others.
But I have also tasted since childhood the full
arc of the past, its cataclysms and wonders.
And sometimes glimpsed the shape of what may come.
I have received much, but ask, as of my death:
"*Will the known world end?*"

This morning early, I woke to splinters of sound
seeming to fall from another sphere.
Is it this which enfolds the Child?
The sounds were perhaps only my heart pounding,
but fragments of silence between heartbeats
called to me. I would not presume to translate
silence, but now my need is great.
In the murmur of ink, may I hear
a new path in the night:

"The Child is the echo of that which masters time,
disintegration of matter. Our matter.
One thing changes into another.
Prayer is in the face of this.
To meet the tremendum, a vortex
of destruction and birth so great
it can only lead to light, is purification.
You must trust what it means to pass through this.
There is everything to fear, and nothing.

"You dwell between worlds, at the very crossroads
of renewal and dissolution. Walk out then
into this day, boldly human,
to see what is hidden in front of you,
hear what is hidden and obey.

"The future is already in your cells:
it awaits your rising. There is a fountainhead
from which past and future unfold,
become known, have always been known.
To which everything returns, unknown.
Grow, beyond thought, to touch this.

"Know that consciousness, never visible,
is greater than prophecy. Small motions
alter the large, but you cannot know how.
Every note in the world must be sounded.
Let each note in yourself be sounded.
Let each note sound, finally, into the void and fullness
the Child has revealed is ours.
Let your greatest work come at the end.

"And may you find what it means to submit,
moment by moment, to unspeakable Love:
that living wind, torchlight
in the living labyrinth,
that sword, vibrating, aimed now and always
at the solitary sheath of your heart.
Unbreakable.

"Caspar, the child in your heart was also you.
Let your spine straighten in remembrance."

THE PEACHES OF IMMORTALITY

—In Chinese mythology, the fruit of peach trees that bloomed every 6000 years was served at a feast that renewed the gods' immortality.

They say, "The fire that becomes known to us
in the trees' brocade,
in the congealing of past and future
where we too are learning to be born,
burns, moves as intimately in you
as the first walk through your kitchen
in early morning, or the child
at hand's reach, or words
heard aloud through an open window.
And this body you will release
shudders and breaks under the spokes
of a music that is its own.
Its own—and the bones can be released.

"We come to your table in the night.
We are close, so near.
But in the unclaimed honey of your hour,
are you willing to be uprooted
into the sky of your heart?
Leave your final dust even now
on the path of your birth?
Be pierced by the bitter skin
of your effulgent seed?"

NOW LET THERE BE EVENSONG, RETREAT

Now let there be evensong, retreat.
Let the deathless seed
be sweet kindling to itself.
Let cold despair, defeat
blow helpless past
the teas and spices patient on their shelf,
the steady fingers working at their task,
awaiting friends to come.

Let deer gather in the clearing.
Let shuttered Being pull its lantern close,
and closer still.
Let it be marveled on
how a simple shawl around the neck
can keep Great Winter back.
How one
lit tea light's artless spine
retrieves the Sun.

Notes

p. 11 *"First Day of School:"* The theme of a young woman with the task of separating out a large pile of mixed grains occurs frequently in traditional stories, in this poem referring to both the Greek myth of Psyche and Eros, and the Russian folktale "Vasalissa the Beautiful."

p. 21 *"The New Roommate:"* Ganesha, in Hinduism, is the elephant-headed god who removes obstacles, a patron deity of sciences and the arts. The *Bhagavad Gita* is a Sanskrit poem central to Hindu thought and spirituality (see note on *"Impartiality"* below).

p. 81 *"Inscription Near the Gate of the Labyrinth:"* The "labyrinth" here refers both to the mythical Labyrinth at Knossos on the island of Crete, and to the no less daunting labyrinth of life on earth, with perhaps cosmic reasons for its difficulties.

p. 49 *"Of Parable and Flight:"* The butterfly has been a symbol of the soul or psyche since ancient times (see also *"Soul and Sacrifice"*).

p. 88 *"A Rose Stands Guard Over the Soul:"* The symbol of the rose is often used in healing work as a indicator and "gatherer" of energies.

p. 94 *"Ireland Journal:"* Carrowmore is a neolithic site of stone circles near Sligo, Ireland, from around the fourth millennium BC. Newgrange, north of Dublin, is also a neolithic monument, from approximately 3200 BC. Glendalough, Wicklow County, was founded by St. Kevin in the sixth century, and was home to a thriving monastic and secular community for over 600 years.

p. 117 *"At Christopher's Passing:"* . . ."he who could see beyond form" referring to Christopher Stewart, medical intuitive and friend, who passed away in 2019.

pp. 123 *"In the Year of Turning Sixty."* The river Styx, in Greek mythology, is the river flowing between the worlds of the living and the dead. It is a river so cold, implacable and immutable, that the gods swear their undying oaths upon it.

p. 121 *"Twilight of the Gods:"* The Norse gods, unlike Greek and other deities, were not immortal. According to the poetic epic *Edda*, the Twilight (or "doom and destruction") of these gods was completed in a huge battle, Ragnorok—very likely a geological cataclysm. In this poem, the Norse gods and elements of modern life overlay each other, as the gods observe their own decline. This is perhaps an indication of how radically world perception changes with the passage of centuries, while the *forces* represented by the gods of ancient times remain what they were.

p. 132 *"The Creator's Sorrow:"* See notes for *"On a New Conception of God'"* below.

p. 140 *"Impartiality:"* Kurukshetra is the battlefield on which the battle at the center of the Indian epic poem *Mahabharata* takes place. This 18-day battle of mythic scale, in which hundreds of thousands of warriors died, was sparked by a dynastic quarrel between royal cousins, some of them sons of the gods. The battle is often said to be the beginning of the modern era, or *Kali Yuga*. It was on Kurukshetra that the spiritual dialogue comprising the *Bhagavad Gita* took place before this battle, between the anguished Arjuna, the warrior-king who does not wish to fight, and his royal kinsman, the god-king Krishna. The quotation accompanying the poem is from *The Bhagavad Gita: A Guide to Navigating the Battle of Life*, by Ravi Ravindra, Shambala, Boulder 2017.

p. 149 *"Suite for Persephone:"* The story of Demeter, Greek goddess of the harvest, her daughter Persephone, and Persephone's abduction into the Underworld by Hades, god of the dead, is well known. But the many "meanings" of Persephone are far from simple. She begins as a "maiden in descent," essentially a victim of rape; she returns to the earth above as both Beauty and Spring, but every year resumes her role in the Underworld as Queen of the Dead, or Dark Goddess. She is the seed which goes underground, to later bear fruit; and she is that which both gives life and takes it away.

Her own journey here is to a kind of autonomy in service of the Whole, passing from the meadows of earth into the halls of death. She mingles with the dead in the Hell of regret, half-completion, experiencing this fully. Then she joins the dead in meditation before returning to earth to both give and take back, in perpetuity.

Probably, the many "meanings" of Persephone cannot be put into words. But one can imagine them as multi-dimensional processes taking place perhaps simultaneously and eternally, and come to feel how all that Persephone represents is to be revered.

p. 178 *"Day in October Near Redwoods:"*

"...don't you know you are All Suns/to our waning light?:" reference to the Ray of Creation, *In Search of the Miraculous*, P.D. Ouspensky, Harcourt, Brace and Co., New York, 1949, p. 82; one Sun (ours) and all others.

"Between Holy God, Holy Firm...:" reference to prayer expressing the "Law of Three," excerpt from *All and Everything, First Series: Beelzebub's Tales to His Grandson*, E.P. Dutton & Co., New York,1950, p. 752:

"Holy God,
Holy Firm,
Holy Immortal,
Have mercy on us."

p. 181 *"Of Jacob and the Angel:"* referring to the Biblical story in *Genesis* of the emergent leader of the Jews at the ford of a river, wrestling all night long with a "man" who refuses to give his name. This being is said, in different sources, to be either God or an angel, and at day-break he gives the defeated Jacob his blessing, and the new name of Israel.

p. 187 *"On 'A New Conception of God:'"* from an excerpt of Philip Mairet's book *A.R. Orage: A Memoir,* a comment by G.I. Gurdjieff that his aim (or "whim") was "to live and teach so that there should be another con-ception of God, a change in the very meaning of the word."

Within these short poems, the term "Prayer and Despair" refers to a deeply moving piano piece composed by G.I. Gurdjieff and Thomas de Hartmann. "Oil spill of the heart" refers to the disastrous Deepwater Horizon oil spill in the Gulf of Mexico, flowing uncontrollably at that time (May, 2010).

"A particle of the sorrow of the Creator?" refers to an excerpt from *All and Everything, First Series: Beelzebub's Tales to His Grandson,* E.P. Dutton & Co., New York,1950, p. 372:

> " *'The factors for the being-impulse conscience arise in the pres-ences of the three-brained beings from the localization of the parti-cles of the "emanations-of-the-sorrow" of our OMNI-LOVING AND LONG-SUFFERING-ENDLESS-CREATOR. . . . And this sorrow is formed in our ALL-MAINTAINING COMMON FATHER from the struggle constantly proceeding in the Universe between joy and sorrow.'"*

"Resourceful, ever-hungry wolf/tender sheep, you follower:"

"Only he will deserve the name of man and can count upon any-thing prepared for him from Above, who has already acquired corresponding data for being able to preserve intact both the wolf and the sheep confided to his care."

". . . the word 'wolf' symbolizes the whole of the fundamental and reflex functioning of the human organism and the word 'sheep' the whole of the functioning of a man's feeling."

—*Meetings with Remarkable Men*, G.I. Gurdjieff, E.P. Dutton, New York, 1974, p. 4

p. 194 *"The Buddha's Palm:"* In the 15th century epic story *Journey to the West*, the Monkey King, seeking immortality, upsets immutable laws of Life and Death with his outrageous misdeeds. Finally, the Buddha himself makes an offer to Monkey. If Monkey can somersault off the palm of the Buddha's hand, he can rule the world; if not, he must return to earth and accept punishment for his wrongdoings. This looks easy for Monkey, but after many cloud somersaults, each taking him more than 33,000 miles, Monkey realizes this is impossible. He is sent to earth and imprisoned for 500 years before taking part in a dangerous journey to bring Buddhist scriptures back to the East.

p. 199 *"Of the Magi:"* There are of course many mysteries enshrouding the three Magi, or three kings who are said to have visited the Christ Child. These deeply learned scholar-kings (or priest-astrologers) are said to have practiced the Zoroastrian faith. One legend says that they all died on or near January 6, 55 A.D., Melchoir at 116, Balthazar at 112, Caspar at 109. Another source paints Melchoir as an aged grey-bearded Arabian king, Balthazar as the swarthy, middle-aged King of Ethiopia, and Caspar, the King of Tarsus (in Turkey), as a young man in his twenties. These poems lean toward this latter source, exploring the Magi as representations of old age, middle age and youth—having encountered a Being greater than what any human thought possible.

p. 204 *"The Peaches of Immortality:"* referring again to the story of the Monkey King (see *"The Buddha's Palm"* above). One of Monkey's transgressions in heaven was consuming almost all the peaches of immortality intended for the gods, which bloomed only once every 6,000 years.

Index of Poem Titles

CPSIA information can be obtained
at www.ICGtesting.com
Printed in the USA
LVHW111735121120
671532LV00017B/446/J